DON'T YOU KNOW THERE'S A WAR ON?

Life on the Home Front During World War II

December 7, 1941, brought about a cataclysmic change to America. The Japanese attack on Pearl Harbor catapulted the country into a global war that everyone expected, but still caught most by complete surprise. And yet, within a matter of months, the country was transformed into the greatest arsenal of war the world had ever seen. Over 16 million men and women served in uniform while nearly four times that number became citizen volunteers on the home front answering their country's call to service.

Don't You Know There's a War On? is a trip down memory lane during those challenging years when an entire nation went to war. Every man, woman, and child was called into service, and few, if any, refused the call.

This book is not just about volunteers and sacrifice. It also tells the story of one of the nation's best kept secrets in the Navy's incredible "V" program, the story of *Stubborn Hellion*, the Japanese "balloon bombs," and the bombing of Oregon by an ingenious Japanese plan.

Don't You Know There's a War On? is a delightful read about those momentous days during World War I' was forever changed b historians describe as the the 20th century.

D1445452

Other books by Edward Steers, Jr.

Escape and Capture of John Wilkes Booth

The Quotable Lincoln

Lincoln. A Pictorial Biography

His Name Is Still Mudd

Blood on the Moon

The Trial

Lincoln Legends

Don't You Know There's a War On?

Life on the Home Front During World War II

Edward Steers, Jr.

SIGN OF THE OX
in association with
THE LEHIGH VALLEY HERITAGE MUSEUM
Allentown, Pennsylvania

Cover and book design by
Kieran McAuliffe

First Edition, November, 2007

ISBN: 978-1-57747-128-8

This book is respectfully dedicated to
Michael F. Hochella
William H. Hochella
Edward Steers, Sr.
and Samuel C. Zeller

Contents

Preface   xi

Introduction   1

ONE   A Date Which Will Live in Infamy   17

TWO   Radio Goes to War   25

THREE   Stubborn Hellion   49

FOUR   The Navy's V for Victory   71

FIVE   Use It Up, Wear It Out, Make It Do, or Do Without   87

SIX   This Is Where We Came In   115

SEVEN   Any Bonds Today?   133

EIGHT   Books Are Bullets in the War Against Fascism   151

NINE   What Can We Do to Help?   167

TEN   June 6, 1944   197

ELEVEN   Victory!   219

Index   239

Acknowledgements

In looking over my notes and various papers that served as background for writing this book, I realized the large number of individuals I am indebted to for their generous help in supplying me materials, advice, and encouragement along the way. I am especially indebted to Kieran McAuliffe and his wife, Celia Lynn. Kieran is responsible for the design and layout of this book. His tireless effort over many months was an indispensable part of making this book possible. Celia Lynn's keen eye and careful editing saved me from numerous errors. Their generous help and advice were immeasurable.

I want to thank Joseph H. Nichols and Albert and Janet Salter, three good friends who graciously read and improved the manuscript.

The staff of Moravian College was helpful in researching the collection of materials housed in their institution. I am especially grateful to Daniel R. Gilbert, Professor Emeritus of History, for reading the manuscript and offering many helpful suggestions. I also wish to acknowledge the help of Jim Tyler, Archivist, and Wendy Juniper, Reference and Public Services Librarian. They cheerfully granted my every request.

I thank the staff of the Bethlehem Public Library: Barbara Suber and Jane Gill, Reference Librarians, for their time and generous help in guiding me through their wonderful resources.

A special thank you goes to my friends and classmates from Hamilton Elementary School. Cinda Jensen and her husband Tom, Edward "Ned" Halteman, Jr., Joanne Rudolph Cacciola, Barry "Butch" Lynch, and Frances "Bing" Van Nuyes were generous in sharing their memories and family photographs.

I especially want to thank Michael F. Hochella and William

World War II. Unit histories abound. There are far fewer books dealing with the home front, and far fewer still dealing with children who lived through those historic years.

To most children, boys in particular, the war years held a certain excitement. The war, in many ways, was heroic to us. The soldiers, sailors, and marines who fought were our heroes, including those who spent their time fighting the enemy on the silver screen and on the printed page. As children, we were generally shielded from the dark tragedies of the war, especially in the beginning years. The media softened the horrors and atrocities, limiting their coverage to events and not to people. War movies were generally sanitized versions of real life. Newscasts, magazines, and newspapers tempered the tragedy of war to a large degree. Yet every one of us knew someone who had lost a loved one to enemy action. Our neighbors who lived in the house across the street lost their only son when his plane went down over Germany in 1944. He was only eighteen years old. The little red and white banner with the blue star so proudly displayed in their front window was replaced by one with a gold star telling all who passed by that their son had died. The flag was a silent message to everyone in the neighborhood of the pride and the anguish of the mother and father who lived there.

As bleak as events were at times, no one doubted that we would win the war. But to do so required the commitment of all of us "to do our part." Everyone was mobilized to contribute in some way on a daily basis. As children, it was our job to collect the everyday materials that previously were part of the nation's trash. We gathered up old newspapers, tin cans, empty shaving cream and toothpaste tubes, along with such unusual items as milkweed, kitchen fat, and tinfoil from cigarette and chewing gum packs. When we were not scavenging our communities or attending school, we were playing war on the back lots in our neighborhoods or living it in the movie theaters we frequented every Saturday morning or afternoon. Heroic figures such as Captain Midnight and Jack Armstrong fought the Axis powers over the radio while Captain America destroyed their armies in the comic books we read. Even such peaceful creatures as Donald Duck and Bugs Bunny became soldiers in the fight to save democracy while the likes of Smilin' Jack and The Bowery Boys tracked down Nazi agents intent on blowing up our factories. Everyone became involved. ·

The final victory over the Axis powers was a joint effort of our armed forces and the men, women, and children on the home front who made great sacrifices while out-producing the rest of the world combined. This book is not meant to be a memoir or a history of the home front during those momentous years. It is, rather, a selection of personal experiences blended with some of the larger events taking place locally and nationally that involved my generation and my parents' generation. Experiences that our children and grandchildren should know more about.

Private businesses often supplied the personnel and advertising in promoting home front themes. The General Motors Corporation distributed this 1942 poster designed to encourage workers to work harder and produce more.

My brother John and me (saluting) with our aunt's two foster children,
Jackie and Bobby, in front of our grandparents' house in Bethlehem.

Introduction

I was born on my mother's twenty-fifth birthday in the front bedroom of our house on Chelsea Avenue in Bethlehem, Pennsylvania. My mother tells me it was a beautiful spring day, which, of course, meant nothing to me, being unaware of the weather or much of anything else at the time. Politicians and preachers and everyday people argue heatedly over the precise moment life begins. To the individual person, life begins with memory – for without memory there is no life to speak of.

My own life begins with my earliest memory, which can be dated to the Christmas of 1940 when I was just beginning to acquire those bits of information tucked away in the recesses of my brain. I can remember sitting in a dark room fascinated by a halo of diffuse red light surrounding an orange center. All around the halo were many different colors that flickered on and off against a black background. The bright colors blinking in the dark formed a beautiful image that became fixed in my memory. There are moments even today when the image flashes in my mind's eye, flickers for a second, then disappears as quickly as it appeared. It leaves me with a pleasant feeling of something that is past but was good. Years later I came to know what I had seen. It was a Christmas wreath made of crinkled red cellophane, the kind that every five-and-ten-cent store carried at Christmastime. In its center was a plastic candle that held an orange-colored bulb. The wreath hung in the big front window of our house during Christmas. At night with the room lights turned off you could see the wreath hanging in the window surrounded by the colorful lights that framed the windows and door of the house across the street. It was a simple image and yet memorable to a young child seeing it for the first time. Sadly, it would be several years before I would see it again. The beautifully colored lights that marked the Christmas season every year would be turned off, a casualty of "blackouts" brought on by war.

I was the third son born to my mother and father. Their first child, a boy, died at birth. My brother John came next in 1934 followed by me in 1937. Thirteen years later, a sister, Mary Beth, was born completing our family. My father was a college professor who taught science at Moravian College and Theological Seminary located a few blocks from our house. My mother was a housewife who occasionally served as a faculty hostess at social functions at the college. Much of our family life revolved around the college where my father had been a student and a faculty member.

All four of my grandparents lived within walking distance of our house, and all of my uncles and aunts (ten uncles and eight aunts) lived in Bethlehem within easy reach. Prior to World War II most families living in small towns and cities like Bethlehem were stable entities. The era of moving about dividing families and scattering them to faraway places was still in the future. Even during the depression years in the 1930s most Bethlehem families chose to ride out the hard times by finding ways to make ends meet without breaking up the home and moving away.

My parents rented the right half of a brick duplex halfway up the block on Chelsea Avenue. The house was owned by Mr. Weirbach, a tight-lipped German who spoke only when necessary, at least when it came to kids. More often than not he would utter a grunt or a nod of his head, greeting us with a wave of his hand. He lived three houses down from us, which made it convenient to pay the rent or, on occasion, to explain why the rent was late. I learned in later years that this was not uncommon since my father worked for a small college that struggled to make ends meet during the depression years. Paychecks were not always on time, a fact that Mr. Weirbach understood and let the monthly rent slide until a check arrived.

Chelsea Avenue was not a very long street. It ran for five blocks and the part where we lived was on a steep hill that was ideal for roller-skating in the summer and sledding in the winter. On days when the snowfalls were heavy the police would show up at the intersection at the bottom of the hill and set up saw horses stringing rope between them to reroute traffic so we could sled without having to worry about getting run over by a car. It really wasn't much of a nuisance factor for the adults on the street since few neighbors owned a car and those who did kept them in their garage most of the time because of gas rationing.

The street was lined on both sides with large maple and sycamore trees whose roots occasionally pushed up sections of the cement sidewalk, making roller-skating a real challenge. The uneven sections of sidewalk were welcomed as a kind of dare by most of the kids who turned it into a slalom course seeing who could negotiate the uneven pavement without falling. It was an era before safety helmets and kneepads. OSHA was still only a gleam in some bureaucrat's eye. Skinned elbows and chipped teeth were a part of the hazards of growing up.

The homes along the street were nicely kept. The occupants regularly swept their small pieces of sidewalk, not wanting to be outdone by their neighbors. Maple trees can be messy, especially in the spring when they start launching their winged seedpods that helicopter to the ground by the thousands. Not many people in our neighborhood owned automobiles. I never remember more than two cars parked on our block at any time, leaving plenty of room for street games. During the war years streets were an important playground for kids. Municipal parks were few and far between. While every neighborhood had an open lot ideal for war games, they were unsuitable for games of finesse. They were better made for games that required holes in the ground where you could hide or small hills you could jump over yelling war cries like "Geronimo!" The old Indian fighter's name was made part of the new vocabulary of war slang by paratroopers who first started yelling the name when jumping out of airplanes during the North African campaign of November 1942.

Neighborhood streets were turned into playgrounds. There were a dozen different games with rules that were adapted to curbs and manhole covers, telephone poles, and overhead wires as boundaries or places to score points. Stick ball, wire ball, and kick-the-can were three of the more popular games. The equipment was easy to come by – an old broom handle (with sticky black tire tape wrapped around one end, making a perfect grip), half of a tennis ball, or an old tin can. The streets were filled with kids running from manhole to curb to tree to pole and back again shouting nonsensical words like "ollie-ollie-in-free." Visiting the old neighborhood sixty years later, the houses and the street have changed little. The curbs and manhole covers and overhead wires are still there – only the children are missing.

The war, like most tragedies, brought people closer together. It was a time when few people were considered strangers. In today's world that attitude is considered dangerous, and we teach our children to avoid strangers and to play only in safe places. Back then we freely ran the streets and roamed through peoples' backyards without being yelled at or chased, which added to the variety of our play world.

The most interesting backyard on Chelsea Avenue belonged to an elderly widow named Lambert. Mrs. Lambert was an English woman who lived next door to Mr. Weirbach. Short and stocky, she seemed ancient with her white hair twisted into a donut-shaped bun on the back of her head. She had a hobbling gait that made her sway from side to side as she slowly plodded along. She seldom spoke but when she did it was with a lovely English accent that we found fascinating.

Running down the middle of Mrs. Lambert's backyard was a long skinny trough set in the ground that was filled with water. It was made out of concrete and the inside had been painted a pale blue. The trough was filled with wispy-tailed goldfish that gracefully weaved their way around the lily plants and arrowroot growing in the pond water. The old lady enjoyed having the younger neighborhood children sit around her pond watching the fish. Occasionally she would hand out cookies along with an admonition to be sure not to let any crumbs fall in the water. It seemed cookies were not good for her fish. When war came she displayed two small flags in her front window, one English, the other American. It reinforced the message that the Brits were our friends.

The homes on Chelsea Avenue had no front yards to speak of, only a few feet of mossy grass between the front of the house and the sidewalk. Most of the houses had large, striped awnings shading the front porch on bright summer days. In the evenings the porch was a cool gathering place for the adults to sit and visit with the neighbors. We had a large Sears and Roebuck Silvertone radio that sat in the living room beneath the front window. I was its constant companion on late afternoons when the airwaves were filled with a string of radio heroes that took me to exotic faraway places and thrilled me with their daring adventures. In wintertime I would sit in the dark room huddled near the radio, the only light coming from the soft yellow glow of the dial. On summer evenings the porch became a convenient place to sit with the window open listening to Fibber McGee and Molly or Charley McCarthy.

My brother John and I shared a bedroom on the second floor in the middle of the house. We slept in twin beds and shared a small dresser and bookcase. A single closet no more than four feet in width set in one corner of the room. The dresser and closet held all of our worldly possessions with room to spare. On each of the headboards Dad had carefully arranged a dozen colorful decals of the mascots of the more popular college football teams of the day. There were high-kicking mustangs (SMU), wily badgers (Wisconsin), golden gophers (Minnesota) and Quakers (Penn). Fordham rams, Boston eagles, yellow jackets (Georgia), mules (Army), goats (Navy), and terrapins (Maryland). Best of all, Dad had pasted on the ceiling above our beds small luminescent stars forming different constellations and planets that were coated with a phosphorescent paint. At bedtime when the lights were turned out the stars gave off a soft greenish glow that twinkled overhead, growing dimmer and dimmer until they disappeared. Staring up at the ceiling as the luminescence slowly faded away invariably resulted in our falling fast asleep. My brother and I learned at an early age of Ursa Major and Ursa Minor, Casseopeia, and of Polaris, the North Star, which sits at the end of the Little Dipper. The star, Dad told us, always marked due north no matter where you happened to be. Its position never changed in the night sky. Should the day come when far from home and lost, the North Star would point the way back. He also told us that in the days before Abraham Lincoln, runaway slaves from the South used the North Star as their guide pointing them north to freedom. Fifty-eight years later the current owner of our house graciously invited me to examine the old homestead. Walking into my old bedroom I looked up at the ceiling hoping that under the many coats of paint I would see the faint outlines of Ursa Major or Ursa Minor. It was hoping for too much.

* * *

The city of Bethlehem represented the industrial heart of the pre-war nation. It was home to the second largest producer of steel in the world, the Bethlehem Steel Corporation. A sprawling giant, the company's mills stretched for four-and-a-half miles along the southern bank of the Lehigh River. World War II ensured steel's role as king, and Bethlehem was its kingdom. At the peak of its operation, in 1943, Bethlehem's steel mills provided jobs to 32,000 employees, including 2,200 women. Nationwide, the company's payroll reached 284,000 employees, including 25,000 women. So successful was the reign of Bethlehem Steel during the first half of the twentieth century that its leaders could not imagine the good times would ever end. But end they did.

By the 1980s, the once mighty steel giant lay crippled, a mere shadow of its former self, barely able to stay alive. Like a beached whale it would thrash vigorously for a moment or two then lay still, desperately trying to stay alive. During the four years from 1981 to 1985, steel companies in the United States lost over seven billion dollars. It was a disaster of major proportions.

John Strohmeyer, the Pulitzer prize-winning editor of the city's only newspaper, the *Bethlehem Globe-Times*, told the story of Bethlehem Steel's dramatic rise and fall in his book *Crisis in Bethlehem*. Strohmeyer wrote that by the end of the war in 1945 the steel industry in the United States out-produced the rest of the world combined in total steel tonnage, and "eighty-five percent of all manufactured goods in the U.S. contained steel in one form or another." Bethlehem Steel would become the single largest manufacturer of war materiel in the world. A few weeks after the attack on Pearl Harbor, Bethlehem Steel had over one-and-a-quarter billion dollars in orders from the military that ranged from bomb castings to entire warships. In 1943, Bethlehem's shipyards turned out 380 ships, exceeding by 15 its chairman's earlier boast that the company would build a ship a day. By war's end it had built over 1,100 ships in the span of 1,300 days. But all this was in the future. The war years were healthy years for both the steel company and the city of Bethlehem.

Bethlehem Steel traced its origins to 1861 when the Bethlehem Iron Company located on the south side of the river (known as South Bethlehem). It soon took hold and grew, and in

1899 was reorganized into the Bethlehem Steel Corporation. As the company grew, so too did the immigrant population that was necessary to its operation. Beginning around 1880, a large Slovak community sprang up on the south side of town drawn by the steady employment and good wages that the steel company provided. By the time of Bethlehem Steel's reorganization in 1899, 70 percent of South Bethlehem's 20,000 residents were immigrants, and of these one-third were Slovaks. The Slovaks were conservative by nature and hard-workers who retained much of the culture they brought with them from the old country. My mother's parents, Andy and Mary Hochella (ho-shell-a) were second generation Slovaks who located on the north side of town rather than in the ethnic neighborhoods across the river in South Bethlehem. But like their Slovak cousins on the South Side, they retained a strong work ethic, much of the language, and most of the recipes handed down from mother to daughter over the years.

Practically every family had someone who worked for Bethlehem Steel or depended on it indirectly. My family was no different. Andy Hochella was a foreman of Maintenance in the Saucon open hearths. My dad's father, John Steers, was a master machinist who spent most of the war planing the rifling for the large guns destined for America's warships. Dad worked alongside his father for a period while he was earning a Master's degree at Lehigh, and my mother, by the end of the war, worked one of the company's switchboards as a telephone operator. The sons and daughters, and later in life, grandchildren, of Andy Hochella and John Steers worked in the steel mills at one time or another. In the 1950s, my brother and I earned our way through college, working at the company's Sparrows Point plant in Baltimore. As summer employees, we earned union wage, and with orders for steel booming in post-war America, we could pull as much overtime as we could physically stand – and at union wages, we could earn enough to pay all of our college bills.

* * *

At the outbreak of World War II, Bethlehem's population was just over 58,000. By the end of the war it had risen to 68,000. The increase was due to the influx of laborers working for Bethlehem Steel. There were 13,500 homes in the city, of which 65 percent were owner occupied. There were six hotels, one senior high school, four junior high schools, and two public libraries. There was one hospital, 72 churches (representing 20 denominations), and one daily newspaper, the *Bethlehem Globe-Times*. The city boasted a university (Lehigh), a college and theological seminary (Moravian), and the second largest steel company in the world.

The city began its life on the north side of the river in 1741. Its midwife was a little known religious group from Eastern Europe known as Moravians. A Protestant sect, the Moravians were part of a larger pietist movement whose origins go back to the fifteenth century and the Unitas Fratrum, or Unity of Brethren, that flourished in Bohemia and Moravia in Eastern Europe. Suppressed during the Counter-Reformation in 1722, the surviving members of the Brethren were given sanctuary on the Saxony estate of a nobleman named Count Nikolaus Ludwig von Zinzendorf. Zinzendorf, a Lutheran at the time, became enamoured with the teachings of the Moravians and joined the sect, becoming a bishop in the year 1737.

The Moravians were evangelicals, which brought them to America in 1735 on a mission to convert the American Indians to Christianity. The first Moravian missionaries to cross the Atlantic made their way to Georgia with high hopes of bringing the gospel to the Indians living in that part of the country. A few years later a small group from the first settlers set out from Georgia, making their way north to Pennsylvania. Arriving shortly before the Christmas season, they established a colony on 500 acres of land located between the Monocacy Creek and the Lehigh River. The year was 1741. Moravian tradition tells the story of Count von Zinzendorf, now a bishop in the church, arriving at the new site on Christmas Eve in time to conduct the Christmas Eve service. The timing of his visit moved Zinzendorf to christen the new colony, Bethlehem.

Although the Moravians were great missionaries carrying the gospel to the uninformed, they were not strong proselytizers and their numbers grew slowly, reaching only 8,000 adherents by the end of their first one hundred years in America. By the outbreak of the Second World War their numbers had reached 50,000, with the majority concentrated in Pennsylvania. While the Moravians never became an influential church movement in the United States, they became a major religious and economic force in Bethlehem.

Education and music remain an important part of the Moravian experience. From the very beginning of their colonization in America, the Moravians afforded education to both sexes equally, and schools were often built along with places of worship. In 1807, the educational arm of the Moravian Church in America received permission from church authorities in Germany to establish a theological seminary to prepare young men for the ministry. Because its curriculum was so much broader in the liberal arts than most non-sectarian schools at the time, they welcomed non-theology students, changing the name of the school to "Moravian College and Theological Seminary."

Moravian College became a major part of my family's life. On graduating from high school in Bethlehem in 1928, Dad enrolled at Moravian College for the fall semester. In 1932, he graduated and enrolled at Lehigh University, located on the south side of town, where he obtained a Master's degree in biology. That same year he joined the Moravian faculty as an assistant professor teaching biology and organic chemistry. Dad remained on the faculty, working his way up to full professor until the fall of 1945 when he entered the University of Pennsylvania, graduating in 1947 with a doctorate in microbiology.

In 1955-56, I spent my freshman year at Moravian before transferring to the University of Pennsylvania. My brother John graduated from Johns Hopkins University in 1956 with a degree in chemical engineering and returned to Bethlehem to work for the steel company in its open-hearth division. In 1960, he decided his real interest lay in medicine and he applied to medical school. Not having the required science courses necessary for admittance, he attended Moravian in 1960-61. In 1973, my sister Mary Beth graduated from Moravian with a degree in Education, and the following year married a Moravian graduate, Gregory Phillian. Moravian College was an important part of our family's life, and it would become an important part of the country's fight against the Axis powers in World War II.

* * *

1941 saw the greatest economic gains for the country since the Great Depression began twelve years earlier. Although nearly 10 million workers were still unemployed nationwide out of a workforce of 56 million, the economy picked up considerably with the government's increased spending for national defense. Japan's invasion of China in 1937 and Germany's attack on Poland in 1939 forced the Congress of the United States to back President Roosevelt's call for mobilization. With the Congress's backing, Roosevelt pumped eight billion dollars into the economy, creating an increase in employment and salaries and bringing an end to the past several years of malaise.

As 1941 entered its last month, the people of Bethlehem were getting ready to celebrate their best Christmas in over ten years. Known as "The Christmas City," Bethlehem was aglow with the glittering lights of the holiday season that traditionally decorated the streets of the downtown area. Store windows were filled with symbols of Christmas and Jolly Old St. Nick. People were filled with the Christmas spirit and optimism for the year ahead. High atop South Mountain, a giant 91-foot electric star shone its light over the city below. Erected in 1937 by Bethlehem Steel, the "Star of Bethlehem" was a symbol of peace that served as a beacon guiding people to the Christmas City. It soon would stir fears of guiding enemy planes intent on destroying the steel mills and city below.

SOURCES

Hugh Bennick, ed., *Revista* (Moravian College Yearbook, 1941).

The *Bethlehem Globe-Times*, June 1940 – December 1946.

Forging America. The Story of Bethlehem Steel (Allentown, PA: The Morning Call, December 2003)

Ralph Grayson Schwartz, *Bethlehem on the Lehigh* (Bethlehem, PA: Bethlehem Area Foundation, 2003).

Richmond E. Myers, *Sketches of Early Bethlehem* (Bethlehem, PA: Moravian College Alumni Association, 1981).

Mark Reutter, *Sparrows Point. Making Steel* (New York: Summit Books, 1988).

M. Mark Stolarik, *Growing Up On The South Side. Three Generations of Slovaks in Bethlehem, Pennsylvania, 1880-1976* (Lewisburg, PA: Bucknell University Press, 1985).

John Strohmeyer, *Crisis in Bethlehem, Big Steel's Battle to Survive* (Bethesda, MD: Adler & Adler, 1986).

W. Ross Yates, ed., *Bethlehem of Pennsylvania. The First One Hundred Years. 1741-1841* (Bethlehem, Pennsylvania: Bethlehem Book Committee, 1968).

W. Ross Yates, ed., *Bethlehem of Pennsylvania. The Golden Years. 1841-1920* (Bethlehem, Pennsylvania: Bethlehem Book Committee, 1976).

The Star of Bethlehem

Erected in 1937 by the Bethlehem Steel Corporation as a gift to the City of Bethlehem, the 91-foot electric star was displayed throughout the Christmas season from atop South Mountain overlooking the city below. Following the attack on Pearl Harbor, the star was turned off and was not turned on again until December 1, 1945.

Bethlehem Steel

Blast furnaces of Bethlehem Steel where basic materials were turned into steel. In 1994 the company shut down all of its blast furnaces and on November 18, 1995 ended steelmaking in Bethlehem. In 2001 the company filed for Chapter 11 bankruptcy protection. In 2003 Bethlehem Steel's assets were purchased by the International Steel Group.

Top: Our house was the right half of this duplex on Chelsea Avenue. *Middle left:* Mom, my brother John (standing right), and I take a break from digging a tank trap at our cabin in the Poconos. *Middle right:* My brother John (left) and me (wearing helmet). *Lower left:* Chelsea Avenue. Our house was midway up the block on the righthand side of the street. *Lower right:* Our dog Skeeter takes a break.

Top: Comenius Hall, Moravian College. *Middle*: Science building where Dad taught and had his office. *Lower left*: Dad from the 1941 yearbook. *Lower right*: Faculty wives hosting a reception for incoming freshmen. Mom is standing second from the right.

RE WAR

ES WAR ON U. S

iated Press)

ne United States and Britain after Japanese bombers had attacked the gr

the opening assault—struck at Ford Island in Pearl Harbor, the U. S. Nav
on Honolulu itself.

nes had also attacked Manila, an Associated Press dispatch from Mar

The Bethlehem Globe-Ti

3,177   BETHLEHEM, PA., SUNDAY, DECEMBER 7, 1941   BY THE WEEK,
                                                                    18 CENTS

Planes Attack H

nila In Stunning

ts Defense   BULLETINS   U. S.-Ja

Operation   All Naval Officers On Leave Called   From 1

7 (AP)—Japanese airplanes today at-   NEW YORK, Dec. 7 (AP)—A naval official, who
d bases at Hawaii and Manila, and Presi- declined to be quoted said today that the Navy Depart-
the Army and Navy to carry out undis-   ment had sent out an urgent call to all officers on leave to   1853—Commodore Parry
for the defense of the United States.   report at once to naval districts in which they are located   1858—U. S. Consul Tow

ordering him to report for active duty. Michael F. Hochella had come to the realization that the U. S. was headed for war whether it wanted to or not. Hochella, unwilling to wait and take his chances with the draft, had signed up for the Army Air Corps' Aviation Cadet Program four months earlier. He passed the tough entrance exam with flying colors. His orders directed him to report to Avon Park, Florida, where he would begin his flight training. On hearing the news, Gil Gillespie knew he had lost a valuable guard from his basketball team.

S O U R C E S

The *Bethlehem Globe-Times*, November 1941 – December 1942.

Lisa Grunwald and Stephen J. Adler. Eds., *Letters of the Century.* *America 1900-1999* (New York: The Dial Press, 1999).

Michael F. Hochella, letters to Edward Steers, Jr., 1977-1979, Author's Collection, Berkeley Springs, WV 25411.

Richard R. Lingeman, *Don't You Know There's a War On? The American Home Front 1941-1945.* (New York: G. P. Putnam's Sons, 1970).

Geoffrey Perrett, *Days of Sadness, Years of Triumph. The American People 1939-1945* (Baltimore, MD: Penguin Books, Inc., 1974).

Barbara McLean Ward, ed., *Produce & Conserve, Share & Play Square.* *The Grocer & the Consumer on the Home Front Battlefield During World War II* (Portsmouth, New Hampshire: Strawberry Bank Museum, 1994).

Radio Heroes
Upper right: Jack Armstrong, the All-American Boy, next to his "Dragon Eye" ring.
Lower left: Jimmy Allen with a pair of wings.

Hot and Perspired, but Cheerful

Upper: "Kunsman's field" converted into a large parking lot after the war. *Middle left*: The back porch on Chelsea Avenue that served as my "control tower" on those days when I flew my plane to school. *Middle right*: Postman Herb Wimmer, "Mr. Sunshine," delivering the mail to Moravian College. *Lower right*: Coloring book featuring The Shadow.

Top: Captain Midnight's special manual containing "charts, codes, and secrets" along with decoder badges from 1941 (left) and 1945 (right). **Below**: Superman comic book (1942) with a Superman pin offered as a radio premium.

Upper left: Captain Marvel Club felt patch (1944). *Upper right:* "Secret Portfolio" offered by the Lone Ranger to his radio pals. *Middle left to right:* Tom Mix battery-operated telegraph (1942). Hop Harrigan, America's Ace of the Airways, "American Observation Corps" patch. Little Orphan Annie Safety Guard whistle and booklet (1942). *Lower left:* Card 37, produced by Gum, Inc. of Philadelphia. The reverse carries a lengthy description of an American fighter pilot after he has bailed out of his burning airplane. The pilot hangs lifeless from his parachute cords while a Japanese pilot machine-guns his defenseless body. The pilot, his chute in tatters, plummets to earth. The chilling scene served to arouse our hatred of the Japanese and stiffen our resolve.

A Japanese ship under attack by a plane from the 500th Bomb Squadron.
(Michael F. Hochella)

THREE

Stubborn Hellion

The day my button arrived is one of those days I'll never forget, much like that first serious kiss with the girl who sat in the front of the class and got all the answers right. Thanks to Terry Lee and good old Mr. Sunshine, I clutched in my little hand a beautiful white button with a blue bulls-eye. Neatly lettered in red around the bulls-eye were the words "North American B-25 Army Bomber." Inside the bulls-eye were the words "Pilot's Mascot." It was a beautiful item to behold! Although I didn't notice it until years later, the button was made of wood, another by-product of the war years.

For the next few weeks the button went everywhere I went, including to bed. I had a special attachment to the North American B-25. When Uncle Mickey (Hochella) reported for duty on December 21, 1941, he was sent by the Army Air Corps to Columbia, South Carolina, to a B-25 Bomb Group. After several months of training, his bomb group was sent to Australia where they became a part of the Fifth Air Force in General Douglas MacArthur's campaign against Japan. Although my own plane was a P-51 Mustang – you can't do belly rolls and loops with a B-25 – Uncle Mickey's plane soon became my favorite.

Most kids were already savvy about the Army Air Corps and its cadre of planes. The 1930s saw a sharp rise in the nation's interest in aviation. Throughout the '1930s barnstorming pilots thrilled spectators with daring feats and introduced paying customers to the thrill of flying. The radio serials in the '1930s and early 1940s reflected the country's interest by featuring hero-flyers like Jimmy Allen, Hop Harrigan, Captain Midnight, and Terry Lee. Young children and teenagers were drawn to both the fictitious and real aviators of the period. By the time the United States entered the war, America's youngest warriors already knew most of the planes in the U. S. arsenal – and several in the enemy's arsenal as well.

Nose art, the colorful decorations painted on aircraft, became commonplace throughout the fighter squadrons and bomb groups in Asia and Europe. Squadron patches soon followed, and imaginative cartoon symbols identified every unit. Nearly every plane sported a name that reflected the character of its pilot and crew. Names like *Bedroom Bandit*, *Chow Hound*, *Lazy Daisy Mae*, and *Hellzapoppin'* were typical of the pride airmen had in their planes. One of the more interesting use of names came from a popular novelty song of the day entitled *Three Little Fishies*. The song had been number one on the music charts in 1939 and was still popular during the war. Like most novelty songs of the period, it had a catchy phrase of nonsense words that went "Boom-boom, dittum-dattum, whattum-choo." The words wound up on the nose of three North American B-25 medium bombers stationed in the South Pacific. Members of the 500th Bomb Squadron's "C" flight (345th Bomb Group), stationed in New Guinea, named their three planes *Boom-Boom*, *Dittum-Dattum*, and *Whattum-Choo*. The nose of each plane was decorated with a large blue and white sailfish dropping a load of bombs from its belly.

Boom-Boom was the first plane assigned to Uncle Mickey when he was leader of C flight. On October 16, 1943, *Boom-Boom* was so badly shot up during a raid on the Japanese base of Wewak on the northern coast of New Guinea that it was removed from service. Three members of the original crew of *Boom-Boom* later died tragically, one in a Japanese prison camp and two when the plane that was taking them on leave to Sydney, Australia, crashed. *Dittum-Dattum* was destroyed when it crashed during takeoff, killing the entire crew.

Uncle Mickey's plane was replaced with a new B-25 he named *Stubborn Hellion*. Decorating the nose of *Stubborn Hellion* was the head of a wild mustang snorting smoke from its nostrils. It was from Uncle Mickey's second plane that I took the name *Stubborn Hellion* for my make-believe P-51.

Mickey wasn't really my uncle. He was my mother's cousin, which made him my second cousin. Mickey's mother died unexpectedly while he was an infant, leaving three children, two boys and a girl. Mickey's father, unable to raise three infant children and work full-time, sent them to his brother Andy's home in Bethlehem. Andy and Mary Hochella had seven children of their own, four girls and three boys, my mother being next to the youngest of the girls. Overnight, my grandmother found herself raising ten children, four under the age of five. Years later my mother told me that her mother welcomed the three children with open arms and never uttered a word of complaint, raising them as her own. Although Mickey, his younger brother Elwood, and sister Ethyl were first cousins to my mother, they grew up as her brothers and sister. Hence Mickey became my uncle.

In the fall of 1940, Mickey was a freshman at Moravian College. He worked hard, scored high in his grades and was a starting guard on the varsity basketball team. Throughout Mickey's freshman and sophomore years, the shadow of war hovered over the country. While most Americans wanted to stay out of the war, Mickey was convinced that war was coming and nothing would stop it. "The war was already raging in Europe," Mickey later wrote me, "and I knew we would be in it soon." Not content to wait to be drafted, Mickey decided to beat the draft and get a jump on the rest of the country. He chose the Army Air

Corps, "because it was the best of the services, and the hardest branch to get into." He enlisted in the summer of 1941 and in the fall returned to school. On December 19, twelve days after Pearl Harbor, he received his call to active duty. His brother Elwood and cousin Billy would soon follow. Before the end of 1942, Mary Hochella would see three of her "boys" go off to war, two in the Air Corps and one in the Navy.

Mickey was ordered to report to Columbia, South Carolina, at the Air Corps Base located on the outskirts of town. After only eleven hours of flying time in a B-25, Mickey was designated an "instructor pilot." The army was on a crash course to get as many pilots in the air as quickly as they could. After several months of training, the 345th was ordered to Australia as part of the Fifth Air Force commanded by Major General George C. Kenney. The four squadrons arrived in Brisbane in May 1943.

By the time the 345th arrived in Australia, the dark days of Japanese conquest had begun to stall. The Allies blunted the Japanese expansion that had been sweeping across the Pacific and were beginning to mount a counter-offensive under MacArthur. MacArthur's plan involved a strategy of "leap-frogging" over certain Japanese strongholds, leaving them behind the Allied advance where they would "wither and die on the vine." MacArthur dubbed the plan "Operation Cartwheel."

From Brisbane, the entire Bomb Group, consisting of 64 planes and 1,500 men, was moved to Port Moresby on the southern coast of New Guinea. For the first few weeks Mickey's squadron was assigned the job of dropping supplies to the Australian troops holding back a Japanese attempt to capture Port Moresby. Had Port Moresby fallen to the Japanese, an invasion of Australia would have been the obvious next step.

Although dropping supplies was an important job, it was not what Mickey and his buddies had signed up for. They were chomping at the bit for combat missions. The group finally got its chance on June 30, when they were ordered to bomb the Japanese positions near Salamaua on the northeast coast of New Guinea. Bigger, more important missions followed close behind.

The Japanese sweep throughout the Southwest Pacific in 1941 and early 1942 resulted in their establishing main supply bases on the islands of New Britain and New Ireland. These two islands, along with several smaller islands off the coast of New Guinea, made up the Bismarck Archipelago. New Ireland was a long, finger-like landmass that lay perpendicular to New Britain, the larger of the two islands. On the northwestern tip of New Ireland was the important Japanese supply base of Kavieng. The Japanese established this base to support their operations all along the northern coast of New Guinea. Their objective was to drive the Allies completely out of New Guinea and back to Australia. Up to this point in the war, everything had been going Japan's way.

The Allied strategy called for an invasion of New Ireland in an attempt to capture Kavieng. MacArthur, however, was committed to pushing on to the Philippine Islands with as little delay as possible. After the fall of the Philippines in early 1942, MacArthur was ordered to abandon his Philippine command and escape to Australia. Chagrined that the United States had failed to protect the Philippines, MacArthur made his famous "I shall return" promise. His words became a rallying cry in the Pacific, and the Supreme Commander meant to keep his promise. Instead of invading New Ireland, MacArthur decided to bypass it entirely and leave Kavieng in his wake, neutralizing it with air power.

On February 15, 1944, the Fifth Air Force launched its biggest mission of the war. Three separate bomb groups, consisting of 151 planes, targeted Kavieng. If successful, the base would never again function as a staging area for the Japanese. It would be little more than a series of smoldering bomb craters.

The mission began with high-level bombing by squadrons of the 14th Bomb Group flying four-engine B-24 Liberator heavy bombers. Next came four squadrons of the 38th Bomb Group flying B-25 medium bombers. Immediately behind the 38th were the four squadrons of the 345th. The men of the 345th were ordered to fly over the target only a few hundred feet off the ground, strafing the warehouse facilities and supply dumps with their 50-caliber machine guns. All of the Groups' planes had been modified by removing the glass "greenhouse" in the nose of each plane, replacing it with a special canopy holding eight forward-firing .50 caliber machine guns. It turned the B-25 into a deadly strafing machine that possessed firepower never before used in aerial combat.

Flying at such low levels made conventional bombing impractical. Because the planes flew so low to the ground, the explosions from standard bombs were too dangerous to the planes trailing behind. To give them time to clear the target, parachutes were attached to the bombs, slowing their descent, thereby allowing the trailing planes time to fly clear of any ground explosions. The ingenious bomb was dubbed a "parafrag" – short for parachute fragmentation bomb. Using parafrags, the 345th was able to strafe at low levels and still deliver a bombload without climbing to high altitudes or risking a second pass over the target.

While parafrags proved effective in allowing the low-flying planes to avoid bombs dropped by the lead planes, it didn't protect the flights from damage caused by explosions on the ground. When the four squadrons of the 345th swept into Kavieng near ground level, several storage depots were already burning out of control. The entire area was on fire and explosions filled the air with black smoke and flying shrapnel from the exploding ammunition and fuel drums on the ground.

Stubborn Hellion was the lead plane for the 500th's four

flights. "A" flight was on *Stubborn Hellion*'s left while "B" and "D" flights followed close behind. The whole area was a fiery inferno with 55-gallon drums of gasoline and other debris hurtling through the air. The black smoke was so thick it made it nearly impossible to see the other planes of "A" flight on Mickey's left. Years later, Bill Cavoli, a member of the 500th, described the mission as a "flight into hell." Sweeping over the target, Mickey turned loose all eight of the nose guns, cutting a swath of destruction in his front. At this level the airmen could see the enemy scurrying on the ground, and the enemy could see the men in the cockpits as they bore down on them. The war had suddenly become very personal.

As Mickey passed over one of the storage depots, he felt a violent shudder as if his plane had been hit by anti-aircraft fire. The waist gunner's voice crackled over the intercom reporting that the left side of the fuselage was ripped open from just behind the wing to the tail as if a giant can opener had run down the side of the plane, stripping chunks of metal from the fuselage. The port engine started racing out of control, spewing oil and hydraulic fluid from beneath the cowling. Shrapnel from the explosions on the ground had hit the plane, ripping gashes in the fuselage and breaking the fuel and hydraulic lines to the port engine.

Mickey instantly knew that *Stubborn Hellion* was in serious trouble. The propeller blades of the port engine had flattened out, creating a tremendous drag that pulled the plane to the left. It took all of Mickey's strength to hold the plane steady. The vibration was so violent that he thought the plane was going to shake to pieces. With its air speed dropping rapidly, *Stubborn Hellion* was dying. The only question was how long it would take before it plummeted to earth.

With the loss of power from the port engine, *Stubborn Hellion* soon fell behind the other planes of the 500th. Clearing the target, *Stubborn Hellion* was suddenly all alone fending for herself.

Mickey attempted to "feather" the port engine by disengaging the propeller blades so they would stop spinning wildly and eliminate the drag that was pulling the plane to the left. No luck. The damaged engine continued to race wildly with the flattened blades pulling hard to its left. Realizing *Stubborn Hellion* was mortally wounded, Mickey notified the crew to prepare for a crash landing at sea. There was no time to try to gain enough altitude to bail out. Mickey's only thought was to get as far away from the Japanese base as possible to avoid capture. The airmen feared capture more than anything. Stories had circulated among the flyers that prisoners were often executed summarily by beheading. The stories were true. The Japanese hated the airmen because of their devastating attacks against Jap installations. Stories filtered back that the Japanese routinely beheaded their captives with utter contempt for the rules governing captured prisoners.

Clearing the target, Mickey steered for open water. He needed to keep the plane in the air as long as he could to get as far away from Kavieng as possible. The vibration from the crippled plane compounded by the drag of the port engine took its toll on Mickey's strength. It was all he could do to hold onto the wheel. A few miles from Kavieng, *Stubborn Hellion* passed so low over a small island that its right wing clipped the top of one of the mango trees. Once on the other side of the island the plane was less than five feet above the surface of the water. Mickey took advantage of the upward thrust from the "ground effect," trying to gain precious distance. Every hundred feet gained was that much farther from possible capture. At the last possible moment Mickey cut the power to the good engine and the plane hit the water bouncing across the smooth surface like a flat stone.

Thirty years later Mickey described the impact: "I lost

consciousness at the instant of impact, or partially lost it as I had some sense of being thrown into the water. I came to, realizing I was going down, away from the light. My shoulder harness and safety belt were still attached to my seat. On impact my seat was ripped loose and it went through the windshield with me still attached to it. I quickly released the harness. The neckpiece of my Mae West was in front of me. I put it in back of my neck and pulled both CO_2s on the Mae West before I blacked out again."

The vest suddenly swelled with CO_2 and began lifting Mickey toward the surface. Just at the moment he thought his lungs were going to burst he broke the surface of the water gasping for air, spitting water from his lungs. Another few seconds and he would have drowned. "My head was back above the surface when I came face to face, at maybe fifty feet, with the B-25. My pilot's seat protected me as the armor plate preceded me through the windshield."

Fifty feet away, *Stubborn Hellion* was sitting on the surface of the water like a wounded bird. Its right wing was high in the air and its left wing partially submerged. The plane was slowly filling with water. Pressure from the water pushed against the rear compartment door, preventing it from opening and automatically freeing the life raft held inside the compartment. Without the raft and its emergency supplies, the crew faced the danger of losing their only means of survival. Gathering his wits, Mickey swam over to the plane and pulled himself onto the right wing. Climbing up the wing, his weight caused the plane to slowly level out in the water, relieving the pressure on the rear hatch. Suddenly, the door popped open freeing the life raft.

Still on the wing, Mickey watched as the inflated raft floated up against the wing not three feet from where he was sitting. He was badly cut about the face and hands but had no broken bones as far as he could tell. Climbing into the raft, he watched *Stubborn Hellion* slip beneath the surface and slowly disappear into the murky depths below.

Treading water on the far side of where the plane had come to rest were four members of his crew. Bright, the co-pilot, and three enlisted men: Stephens, Lambert, and Kellar. Bright appeared to be unhurt, but all three of the enlisted men were badly injured. Missing was the navigator, John Howard. Mickey suddenly realized that Howard must still be trapped in the plane. Pulling off his Mae West he shouted to Bright, pointing down in the direction of the sunken plane. Both men dove into the water, frantically swimming down to where the plane had settled on the ocean floor. The water was too murky to see more than a few feet, and despite repeated dives they were unable to find the sunken plane. After the third dive the two men realized it was too late to save Howard. They turned their attention to the injured crewmen floating several feet away. Mickey and Bright pulled themselves into the raft and paddled over to the men struggling to stay afloat. All three were too badly injured to climb over the side of the raft, so Mickey had them grasp onto the rope that ran around the raft's edge while he and Bright paddled toward a clump of trees seventy-five yards away.

Reaching the edge of the small island, they found the vegetation so dense they were unable to penetrate it. With the raft pushed tight against the vegetation, Mickey and Bright carefully helped the injured men into the raft. Off in the distance they could see fires burning brightly at Kavieng. They could tell the destruction was considerable. As they watched the glow from the fires, the five men huddled in the raft and waited for the safety of nightfall. Above, a Jap scout plane was circling the area looking for downed airmen.

After a few passes, seeing no one below, the plane left and headed back toward its base. Off in the distance Mickey could see the familiar shape of a Navy PBY seaplane landing in the choppy waters off Kavieng while Japanese shore guns pounded away trying to sink it. He watched the plane take off only to land again and take off again. Once, twice, three times he saw the plane take off only to return and land again. Either it was having engine trouble or it was trying to pick up downed airmen. Hopefully it would come for them next. But hope faded as Mickey and his crew watched the plane take off one last time and slowly disappear over the horizon heading in the direction of their home base on New Guinea.

Darkness finally came. There would be no more Jap patrols until daylight. The situation had worsened, however. The constant rocking of the life raft made it painful for the three injured crewmen. Mickey had used up the small supply of morphine from their first aid kits. It was essential to get the men to land where they could rest without the pain caused by the ocean swells. In the moonlight, Mickey and Bright could make out the white edge of what looked like surf breaking on a beach three hundred yards away. The two men decided to try to reach the beach in hope of getting their injured buddies on land.

Paddling as gently as they could, the crew of *Stubborn Hellion* finally reached the sandy beach just as dawn was breaking. Mickey and Bright hid the raft along with the three wounded men in the high grass just beyond the water's edge. With the injured men resting quietly and the raft safely out of sight, Mickey and Bright bedded down and waited in the hope that someone from their squadron had seen them go down.

* * *

Back at the 500th's base, *Stubborn Hellion* and her crew were listed as missing. Several of the pilots recalled seeing two planes from the 500th go down, but not Mickey's. No one knew what had happened to *Stubborn Hellion*. The men could only hope that it had made it to open water and the crew was still alive.

The following day, the 500th was sent out to search for and destroy a Jap convoy that was heading for Kavieng. Unable to find the convoy, the 500th attacked a small group of supply ships anchored offshore. After dropping their bombs, the squadron headed back to their base. Keith Dougherty, a close friend of Mickey's, radioed the flight leader that he wanted to check out a hunch he had. Leaving the squadron, Dougherty headed toward a small group of islands to the northwest of Kavieng where he hoped to find the missing crew. Flying close to the water, Dougherty buzzed several of the small, mango tree islands. It was getting late and he was running low on fuel. Dougherty decided to make one last pass over the small island where Mickey and his crew were hiding. Suddenly Dougherty caught sight of a man pushing a raft into the surf and waving at the plane. Making a wide turn, he made a second pass directly over the man. It was Mickey waving wildly at the B-25. Circling back over the beach, Dougherty dropped a survival box in the water just off shore then headed back to the base with the good news. The next day, a Navy PBY, with Doughterty on board as their guide, picked up Mickey and the other crew members. They had survived for two-and-a-half days in Jap-held territory and felt lucky to be alive.

For Mickey, it was his 45th combat mission, and, although short of the required 50 missions needed to rotate back home, his harrowing experience more than made up for the difference. After a brief stay in an Australian hospital, Mickey was on a plane headed back to the states and Bethlehem.

* * *

Three months after Mickey's rescue, I was playing in the backyard of my grandmother's house on Goepp Street. My brother was sailing a model airplane from a third-story window to the yard below. My job was to retrieve it and run it back up three flights of stairs to where my brother was waiting to launch another flight. Suddenly, I heard the distinct sound of a plane in the distance. Most kids during the war became skilled at identifying

Allied and Axis planes from their silhouettes. Some kids could even distinguish planes by their sound. I wasn't one of them. I stood in the yard listening as the sound grew louder and louder. Suddenly an enormous roar filled the air over my head as a beautiful B-25 passed directly over the house. It was so close to the ground I could feel the vibration in my body as it roared past me.

In another instant my mother popped through the kitchen door. She was pointing toward the sky and I could hear her yelling, "It's Mickey! It's Mickey!" When I asked her later how she knew it was Mickey she said he was the only pilot crazy enough to buzz a residential neighborhood. The plane climbed high in a long sweeping arc and slowly turned back toward the house to make a second pass. In another minute the plane roared over our heads so close I could have hit it with a stone. By now several of the neighbors were out of their houses, pointing and waving wildly at the olive drab plane as it headed toward the horizon "wagging" its wings in the pilot's universal symbol for "hello." Years later, digging through the Moravian archives, I found an item in one of the campus newsletters that told of Mickey's return: "Captain Mickey Hochella paid a visit to our campus this week. He flew over the campus and gave a final greeting to all those who were watching his plane circle overhead."

"That wasn't the half of it," Mickey told me later. "I buzzed the Hill to Hill Bridge and Bethlehem Steel," he said with a twinkle in his eye. "Funny thing, one of Aunt Mary's daughters was working in the steel company's main office on the South Side – she later told Aunt Mary that she looked out her eighth-story window, DOWN, as I went flying by." Mickey later recalled a phone call he received the next evening from an executive at Bethlehem Steel, complaining about his "dangerous" buzzing of their buildings: "Some people didn't believe the war was still on. I simply told the guy I was on a training flight; thanks for calling and see you later." Then, throwing out his chest, he said, "We were trained to be tigers. Hell, we were all tigers in those days. You damn sight better be, or you wouldn't last very long." Uncle Mickey had come home in grand style.

I have no recollection of being driven to the airport that afternoon, but I remember everything that followed like it happened only yesterday. My brother and I stood gawking out the large glass window of the terminal lobby. We couldn't believe our eyes. Sitting off on one of the tarmacs was a magnificent North American B-25 Mitchell bomber. Uncle Mickey had commandeered one of the stateside B-25s used for training and flew it the last leg of his journey home to Bethlehem to visit his folks. He had been gone for nearly three years. The excitement of seeing the plane had distracted me from everything else that was taking place. When Mickey finished shaking hands and hugging all the relatives, he looked down at my brother and me and said something about how we had grown since he last saw us. Actually, I had no memory of him at the time of his enlistment. I was too young. But both my mother and grandmother Hochella had photographs of him that they kept on display. The March 3, 1944, *Globe-Times* carried a picture of Mickey on the front page along with the story that he had been missing in action, but was rescued and convalescing – at an address unknown.

Now Mickey was back in town. He looked like he had just stepped out of a Milton Caniff comic strip. He had on a leather A-2 jacket with a white silk scarf around his neck and the traditional "crush" hat tilted back on his head the same cocky way that Terry Lee and his buddies did.

"How would you guys like to see my plane?" he asked. My brother and I were speechless. I remember Johnny opening his mouth but no sounds came out.

We didn't have to say a word. Mickey already knew the answer. "Come on, I'll show you what a great plane looks like."

Mickey walked us out to where the plane was sitting on the runway. It was just the three of us. The closer we got to the plane the bigger it looked. We were about to experience one of those memorable moments in life. As we reached the plane I thought I could hear my mother's voice faintly calling out behind us, "Be careful. Don't shoot your eye out!" It was a universal expression of all mothers who had sons. It was their number one fear next to losing their ration books. To believe Mom, you'd think the country was populated with several million one-eyed men.

Mickey walked us around the plane pointing out different things. Then he asked if we would like to climb inside. The B-25 had two hatches in its belly. One directly beneath the cockpit and a second hatch near the midpoint of the fuselage where the waist guns were mounted. Mickey pulled down the hatch and boosted my brother and me up the small ladder into the belly of the fuselage. Once inside, we climbed forward on our hands and knees into the front part of the plane. My brother climbed into the co-pilot's seat while Mickey boosted me onto the gunner's seat in the top turret. I remember how surprised I was. The seat was nothing more than a bicycle seat mounted on a steel pole – one size fit all. The Plexiglas turret held two large .50 caliber machine guns that were locked in place and couldn't be moved without the power being on. It was lucky the power was off because I felt a sudden urge to grab the twin triggers and start firing away at the other airplanes sitting out on the runway. For a moment I thought I saw a large meatball on the side of one of the fuselages. While Mickey sat in the pilot's seat showing my brother the various workings of a cockpit, I held onto the machine gun blasting one Jap Zero after another from the sky.

The rest of the day is pretty much a blur. That evening Mickey came over to our house on Chelsea Avenue for dinner. The thrill of climbing inside the B-25 has dulled my memory to the events of that evening except for one thing that I still remember. After dinner Mickey reached in his pocket and pulled out a coin. He handed it to me and said I could keep it. I stared down at the large brown coin, slowly turning it over. It was about the size of a half-dollar and made of copper. On one side was the head of a man, and on the other side was a large kangaroo. It was an Australian penny that Mickey still had from his stay in Sydney. The large penny became my prized possession along with my "Pilot's Mascot" button. Unfortunately, the coin and button disappeared somewhere along the way along with my comic books and baseball cards. Years later I was able to buy another coin and button over the Internet exactly like the two I lost. Every now and then I wonder if that beautiful Australian penny is still out there sitting in some kid's sock drawer next to a stack of baseball cards – my baseball cards!

After sitting inside a real B-25 medium bomber, I would never fly my P-51 Mustang again. Ever since that incredible day in the summer of 1944, my first and only choice for the duration of the war was the North American B-25 medium bomber.

By the way, remember that offer Terry Lee made about photographing your name onto microfilm and sending it to the pilot of a B-25 somewhere in the Southwest Pacific? Forty years later, at a reunion of the 500th Bomb Squadron that I attended as Mickey's guest, I asked several other pilots if they ever received a roll of microfilm from Terry Lee with instructions to carry it on a bombing mission. They all shook their heads. Not one of them knew what I was talking about. My undying faith in Terry Lee and his buddies was shaken. I simply couldn't believe they would lie to me. Do you suppose the microfilm got lost in the mails? Or worse yet, intercepted by some Japanese spy?

Kavieng after the first air strike by the 38th Bomb Group (Michael F. Hochella).

Aerial view of the Japanese airdrome at Kavieng. (U.S. Air Force Photo 23457)

Naval officers in charge of the V-5 program standing in front of Colonial Hall on the Moravian College campus. *Left to right:* Lt. Commander McEndy, officer in charge of the Naval Air Cadet Selection Board, Philadelphia. Lieutenant R. Robinson, officer in charge of the University of Pennsylvania Cadet Flight Program. Lieutenant Carl Johnson, Executive Officer for Lieutenant Robinson, Lieutenant Robert E. Fatherly, Reserve Naval Officer in charge of the Cadet Program at Moravian College. *(Moravian College Archives)*

FOUR

The Navy's V for Victory

Thumbtacked to the walls of our bedroom were several large black and white poster-size photographs of Navy fighter planes. The pictures were issued by the Navy's Bureau of Aeronautics for recruiting purposes. There were Grumman Avengers flying in echelon, carrier-based Navy Wildcats, an SBD Douglas Dauntless dive-bomber that gained fame at the battle of Midway, the Marine Corps' gull-winged Corsair, and a PBY Catalina flying boat. Hanging from the ceiling, in the spaces between my father's constellations, were a dozen or so three-dimensional plane models made out of stiff black cardboard. The photographs and the plane models made our bedroom look like a training center for plane spotters. The Navy gave Dad the posters because of his job as a pre-flight instructor in a unique training program that came to Moravian College in early 1943. One of the least known programs that helped win the war, and at the same time saved many small colleges from bankruptcy, was the Navy's "V Program."

In the years immediately preceding World War II, Moravian College experienced financial difficulties typical of many small schools during the Depression. In 1940 the school was running a $48,000 deficit due, in part, to its policy of giving full scholarships to anyone entering the ministry and charging only $100 for tuition to the sons of Moravian clergy. The generous practice helped to deplete the school's endowment fund, putting it in the red. The college needed to change its policies or find more paying students if it were to survive.

The start of the 1941 academic year brought a certain optimism. The incoming freshman class of 70 students was the largest in the school's history. The increase in paying students coupled with donations from the alumni went a long way to help eliminate the deficit. But the relief was only temporary. There were more serious financial problems ahead. Four months into the academic year the Japanese attacked Pearl Harbor. Devastating as it was, it proved to be another blow to many of the nation's small colleges, especially Moravian. With the draft in full swing, three-fourths of Moravian's student body was eligible to be called into service, and the likelihood of that happening was high.

Although the 1942 freshman class topped that of 1941, the college's total enrollment dropped. The number of students continued to drop as students decided to enlist. Most draft-eligible students knew their college days were limited and wanted to choose their own branch of the military rather than be drafted into the army. By the end of the spring semester, the number of students dropped to roughly half the number that started the year. The drop resulted in another financial crisis for the school. The trustees decided their only choice was to reduce the number of faculty. Twelve of the twenty full-time faculty members were let go, bringing the faculty to a low of eight teachers. Fortunately, Dad was one of the teachers retained.

As a result of reducing the teaching faculty, the number of courses dropped from 72 to 54. The retained faculty had to take on courses that were previously taught by those faculty members let go. As if the drop in student enrollment was not bad enough, the summer semester saw enrollments fall even farther, from 172 at the start of the year to 53 at the end. Just as things seemed the bleakest, help came from an unexpected source – the United States Navy. Short on training facilities for its officer-candidate programs, the Navy turned to the nation's colleges and universities for help.

Following the attack on Pearl Harbor, the Navy undertook an

family, the "t" was dropped, softening the name to "Bunny." As a young child, when it was time to go to bed, it became the custom with Mom and Dad to tuck me in with a "Bunny hug" before lights out. I remember an incident on one of those evenings when several of the cadets were visiting the house. When it was bedtime, my brother and I were hustled off to our "squadron room." When it came time for the required "Bunny hug" I protested vigorously, telling my mother I wouldn't go to sleep until I got "Bunny hugs" from everybody. Mom went downstairs and gave the order, and the cadets dutifully obeyed. One after another I received a bunny hug from each of the cadets. In looking back I realize the uncertainty of the times brought everyone a little closer. One could never be certain what tomorrow would bring and the little everyday things, like bunny hugs, were now just a little more important.

One day while the cadets were outside practicing semaphore, a small, brown mongrel dog showed up and joined the group. He began following the cadets around the campus, refusing to "shoo." The dog even showed up outside the classrooms and would curl up outside the door waiting for the cadets to emerge. The dog had obviously adopted the cadets and wouldn't let them out of his sight. It didn't take long before he was following the cadets everywhere, including the shuttle bus that transported them around the campus to outlying buildings. Left outside the dormitory, the dog howled continuously until one of the cadets would break down and take him inside. They eventually adopted the mutt, naming him "Brownie." It didn't take long before Brownie was given free run of the campus as he followed the cadets through their daily routine. He often attended classes with the cadets and if inadvertently left outside a classroom he would scratch at the door until admitted into the room. Brownie was passed from one outgoing class to the next incoming class. Brownie's special status came to an abrupt end in August 1944, when the last cadre of the cadets shipped out. The last cadet to leave was given the unhappy chore of dropping Brownie off at the local dog pound, where he became another casualty of war.

* * *

The Navy's V programs tapped into some of the brightest and best young men the country had to offer. Many of the Navy's V graduates went on to greater success in later life. A total of twenty-one V-12 cadets reached flag rank (Admiral) without the benefit of attending the Naval Academy. Seventeen achieved flag rank after attending the Naval Academy and fifteen reached field rank in the Marine Corps. The V graduates who went back to civilian life after the war included such prominent men as Brock Adams (Secretary of Transportation), Howard H. Baker (U.S. Senate Majority Leader), Robert F. Kennedy (U.S. Attorney General and Senator from New York), Melvin Laird (Secretary of Defense), Pierre Salinger (Presidential Press Secretary under President Kennedy), Daniel P. Moynihan (Senator, New York), Charles "Mac" Mathias, Jr. (Senator, Maryland), Harry R. Hughs (Governor, Maryland), and Edward J. King (Governor, Massachusetts).

Those who later distinguished themselves in the field of education were Martin G. Abegg (President, Bradley University), Robert McCormick (Secretary, Smithsonian Institution), Vernon R. Alder (President, Ohio University), Arthur G. Hanson (President, Purdue University), James Hestor (President, New York University), Raymond C. Baumhart (President, Loyola University), James H. Zumberge (President, University of Southern California).

Graduates who distinguished themselves in the field of athletics were George Allen (professional football), Angelo Bertelli (Heisman Trophy winner), Alvin Dark (professional baseball), Elroy Hirsch (professional football), Bowie Kuhn (commissioner of baseball), Al Rosen (professional baseball), Otto Graham (professional football), Frank Leahy (football coach of Notre Dame), Eddie Erdlatz (football coach of the Naval Academy), Jim Tatum and Forest Evashevski (football coaches at the University of

Moravian Class of V-5 Naval Cadets. (Moravian College Archives)

Navy V-5 cadets during an examination in one of the basement classrooms in Comenius Hall. (Moravian College Archives)

Poster published by the Office of War Information in 1943,
urging people to use up existing clothing.

FIVE

Use it up, wear it out, make it do, or do without.

If you don't need it, DON'T BUY IT.
War Ration Book Two

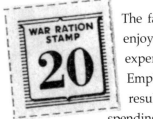

The fall of 1941 found the American people enjoying a prosperity they had not experienced in over twenty-five years. Employment and wages were on the rise, resulting in an increase in consumer spending. At the same time, the war in Europe created such a demand for war materials that shortages began appearing in certain consumer products even though we were not at war. On the other side of the globe the success of the Japanese in Asia cut off the United States's access to rubber. Other imports fell sharply as a result of conquest and the sinking of ships that carried goods destined for the American market. These losses, coupled with the conversion of many factories to war production, resulted in the scarcity of certain products and the outright elimination of others even before we were at war. Manufacturers of rubber bathing caps, sewing machines, and automobiles converted their factories to producing life rafts, machine guns, and tanks.

Shortly after we entered the war in December 1941, the government came to the conclusion that across-the-board rationing was the only way to insure an equitable distribution of the limited goods available to the civilian market. Along with rationing came price controls. It only stood to reason that if goods were in short supply the demand would drive up prices, resulting in spiraling inflation. The government's answer was the Office of Price Administration (OPA), a new agency that Congress gave the authority to ration goods and to set the maximum price that merchants could charge for most commodities (ceiling price). The new system required the government, manufacturers, merchants, and, above all, consumers to work together if an equitable distribution was going to be successful.

Rationing, more than anything else, defined the Second World War to those living on the home front. Americans were not used to the idea of the government controlling the price and distribution of goods. Government regulation of a free market was un-American and smacked of socialism. Nonetheless, the American people were willing to do whatever was necessary to bring victory even if it meant allowing the government to take over the economy, but only while a national emergency existed.

Rationing required an extensive program of controls that reached from the highest levels of government down to each individual consumer. To make a rationing program truly effective, individuals had to play the most important part in the system. Allocations were established for every man, woman, and child, requiring a process that would insure an equitable distribution and, at the same time, allow for exceptions. To do this, the government created "ration boards" and appointed individuals from each community to oversee the rationing program at the local level. The idea was neighbor rationing neighbor. Who better to assess your needs than the person next door?

Congress, the ultimate authority for rationing, gave Roosevelt broad executive power to establish rationing procedures. Roosevelt, in turn, delegated rationing authority to the War Food Administration (WFA) for foods, and the War Production Board (WPB) for all non-food commodities. The responsibility for carrying out the day-to-day process of rationing was delegated to the OPA. When a particular agency (the WFA or

WPB) decided it was necessary to ration a product, it told the OPA to carry out the rationing.

Tires were the first of the commodities to go to war. Tire rationing went into effect on December 30, 1941, three weeks after Pearl Harbor. Passenger automobiles followed in February 1942. Sugar (nationwide) and gasoline (in the Eastern United States only) came next in May 1942. Seven months later gasoline was rationed for the entire country. In March 1943, meat, lard, shortening, oils, butter, margarine, cheese, dried fruits, and all processed foods, whether canned, bottled or frozen, joined the list. Canned milk was added in June 1943, and jams, jellies, and fruit butters joined the list in November 1943. Items like bread, cake, and candy were not rationed, but because the ingredients that were used to make them were rationed, their availability was limited.

Rationed items required "points" in addition to the usual cost in dollars and cents. For example, an item might cost thirty cents and require eight ration points. You might have the thirty cents but if you didn't have eight ration points left in your ration book you were out of luck. Each person was allotted so many ration points, which they could spend as they chose within the major food groups. There was not enough of every individual item to insure equal distribution, but since consumer preferences varied, the point system balanced available supplies with consumer demand. In most cases, if a certain favorite item was no longer available, a substitute generally was – you like carrots, I like peas.

There were four types of rationing control to insure an effective program. The first was "point rationing" where every individual (man, woman, and child) received a certain number of points that could be used at the consumer's discretion. The second was referred to as "uniform coupon rationing." In this instance, coupons were issued for a single commodity (shoes, for example) where everyone shared equally. The third was "differential coupon rationing" where everyone did not share equally, but received coupons based on need (gasoline, fuel oil). The fourth type of rationing required a special "certificate." Certificates were used for the one-time purchase of single items based on a demonstrated need (tires, automobiles, stoves).

Ration "currency" came in several forms. Stamps and coupons were used where everyone participated, and commodities were purchased in small units. Certificates were used where individual requests were evaluated based on need and granted (or denied) based on merit (tires, for example). Major suppliers of goods, including manufacturers and wholesalers, were given "ration bank accounts." As with regular bank checking accounts, ration checks written by a supplier were debited against the points in a supplier's bank account.

* * *

In May 1942, five months into the war, the government issued War Ration Book One, a folded piece of paper that contained twenty-eight consecutively numbered stamps. Because stamps were not transferable, they were removed in the presence of the vendor and each ration book had a description of the owner written in the book to insure they were used only by the authorized person. For example, Mrs. Florence D. of Jackson, Michigan, was described in her ration book as "Height: 5 ft. 3 in., Weight: 140 lbs., Color of eyes: Brown, Color of hair: Brown, Age: 36 yrs., Sex: Female." Identification was a critical part of rationing, but was not a problem in most instances since local grocers knew most, if not all, of their customers.

Ration Book One carried a warning on the front of the book that stated that anyone convicted of violating the "Rationing Orders and Regulations" could be sentenced to ten years in prison and fined up to $10,000. Because ration books could not be transferred, procedures were in effect to handle unused portions of a book. In the event a person left the country or died, the ration book must be turned into the ration board immediately.

The back of Ration Book One contained an oath whereby the owner swore to observe all regulations and that the information provided by the owner of the book was accurate. By the time Ration Book Two was issued, the warning was reduced to a small area equal to a fifth of the front of the book. Ration Book Three limited the warning notice to a small box one-and-a-half inches square on the front cover, while Ration Book Four carried the simple warning stating: "It is a criminal offense to violate rationing regulation." It was clear that the overwhelming majority of Americans played fair and abided by the rules.

Book One was issued initially to ration sugar, already in short supply by May 1942. The Philippines had been a prime supplier of sugar to the U.S. market, and when it fell to the Japanese in early 1942, the sugar supply dropped dramatically. Rationing was able to help insure an equitable distribution of the sugar that was on hand. Incredibly, the government asked people to declare how much sugar they had on hand before they were issued their new ration books. The appropriate number of stamps were then removed from Book One to account for the sugar "on hand." Of course, such a system relied on the honesty of the individual, and to a large extent, individuals were honest. Even had they lied about how much sugar they had on hand, it would have had little effect on the distribution of existing and future sugar.

The very nature of a program designed to regulate the distribution of goods was open to all sorts of illegal activity. Certain items could be purchased without ration points (always at higher than OPA ceiling prices) from "black marketeers." Items such as bobby pins, nylon stockings, gasoline, cigarettes, steak, and liquor were often available through the black market if you knew the right person and had the money to pay the black market price. On more than one occasion I remember overhearing my parents refer to a local butcher as dealing in black market meats. It was not only unfair, but also unpatriotic. They refused to do business with him, which had no impact on his illegal business, but made my parents feel better about their patriotism.

The OPA estimated that four percent of the money spent on food went to black marketeers. This translated to a whopping 1.2 billion dollars annually. To prevent this "black market" activity, the OPA was given authority to enforce its controls and a staff of approximately 2,500 investigators to monitor the rationing process. During its existence, the OPA investigated 305,000 complaints of black marketeering. Of these, 11,000 were considered serious enough to warrant prosecution. Of the 11,000 cases, 10,450 resulted in conviction.

Rationing was controlled through rigorous accountability. The movement of ration currency was accounted for at every transaction from the originator of a product to the consumer and back again to the originator. For instance, a housewife receives stamps from the OPA through her ration board. She transfers the stamps to the retailer (grocer) when she makes a purchase. The retailer then transfers the stamps to his supplier when he replenishes his stock. The stamps then move from supplier to supplier until they reach the primary supplier (manufacturer) who returns the stamps to the OPA, accounting for his sales.

The ration currency returned by the primary supplier must equal the amount of rationed goods he distributed. This system of accountability, dubbed the "Flow-Back System," required that any movement of product be matched with the appropriate ration currency in the opposite direction. As goods moved "down stream," ration currency moved "up stream."

Initially there was no provision for making change in using your stamps. Instead, consumers were urged to plan carefully and use their higher value stamps first, reserving their

Masonic Temple. The OPA office considered the banquet a non-essential event, probably as an example of how tough they were going to be in enforcing the new rule. The police took down the license plate numbers of all the cars and turned them over to the ration board where the owners had to plead their cases. When a reporter for the *Globe-Times* questioned Bethlehem's police chief, Ernest Stocker, about the enforcement, Stocker said that several people had called him directly asking if they could drive to the banquet and were told an emphatic No! (Nix kumm raus)!

The OPA wasn't all bad, however. Despite the harsh crackdown on pleasure driving, they granted the athletic departments of Pennsylvania schools a special exemption, allowing the transportation of athletes and necessary school officials, including referees and umpires, to use their cars to drive to away games. The exemption included coaches, principals, faculty directors and faculty "scorers." But, the OPA warned, spectators could not accompany school officials to the games. Ed Wicht, the secretary of the Pennsylvania Interscholastic Athletic Association, breathed a huge sigh of relief, telling reporters there was no doubt in his mind that the ruling saved interscholastic athletics from completely collapsing under the previous rule.

By the summer of 1943, travel restrictions eased somewhat with the OPA approving vacation travel, but only with prior authorization. Motorists filled out a special form listing their destinations and dates of travel, speedometer readings, makes of car, and license plate numbers. If approved, the form was returned to the applicant with a special authorization stamp and the reviewing agent's signature penned over the stamp. The applicant was required to have the approved form with him when he traveled to avoid receiving a citation for unauthorized travel.

At the same time the OPA cracked down on pleasure driving, the ODT issued an order to the Bethlehem War Transportation Committee to reduce the number of trolley and bus stops, thereby saving fuel used by accelerating and decelerating at each stop. The Lehigh Valley Transportation Company (LVT) complied by eliminating 34 trolley stops and 31 bus stops. At the same time, special "Victory Stop" signs were posted at the remaining stops reminding residents "the fewer the stops the sooner victory."

* * *

The necessity of having to ration food and war-dependent materials such as rubber and gasoline was accepted by the majority of Americans, but doctors were another matter. Strange as it seems today, even doctors came under a form of rationing. The government needed doctors for the military, but so did the civilian population. In calling doctors into military service, the government went out of its way to assure people that the utmost care would be taken to make sure doctors were distributed throughout the country where needed so that no one, civilians or soldiers, would be without adequate medical care.

Footwear and clothing also came under government regulation. War Ration Book Three, issued in July 1943, was initially meant to be used for rationing clothing. Clothing, however, was never rationed, but the raw fibers needed to manufacture clothing were. Leather shoes and boots, as well as rubber footwear, however, were rationed.

Three of the four natural fibers, wool, cotton, and silk, were in high demand by the military. In the case of cotton, scarcity was caused by the fact that there were not enough carding machines to process the raw cotton needed for manufacturing clothing. The synthetic fibers, nylon and rayon, rounded out the list of essential materials needed for war.

As the synthetic fabrics made from nylon and rayon moved from the civilian market to the military, new experimental synthetics were being developed for civilian use. None of them were very good and none of them lasted. One such product was called "Aralac," a fabric made from casein, the principal protein found in milk. The fibers harvested from the bark of redwood trees were used in combination with wool fibers in an effort to extend the limited amount of wool that was available. Reprocessed wool once again emerged as a by-product of war. During the Civil War (1861–1865) uniforms and blankets were routinely made from wool that was recycled by shredding second-hand woolen items and reweaving the harvested fibers into a new fabric. The shredding process, however, broke down the reclaimed woolen fibers into short lengths, making the new yarn weaker and of poorer quality than the original yarn. The fabric made from reprocessed wool was known during Civil War times as "shoddy." Because clothing made from shoddy often fell apart under normal use, the word took on a new meaning: "cheaply imitative, inferior, or poorly done."

Wool was the one fiber that always seemed to be a problem in the public mind. During World War I there was a constant shortage of wool. The military never had enough wool for its uniforms. This memory lingered and prior to World War II the public acted on its own. The year before Pearl Harbor, Americans began buying wool clothing at an abnormally high rate. Although wool was never rationed, the WPB wasn't going to take any chances and issued an order banning the manufacture of full skirts, knife pleats, and patch pockets on all women's clothing. The WPB played no favorites. It also banned men's three-piece suits (no vest) and the extra pair of pants normally sold with men's suits. Lapels were narrowed and patch pockets and cuffs were banned. The result came to be known as the "Victory Suit," a style that turned out to be popular and soon became the standard for men's suits, surviving to this day.

Shortages affected both sexes, although not always equally. Women were the hardest hit because their wardrobe requirements were generally more extensive and many of their undergarments contained rubber or latex. Manufacturers were forced to come up with rubberless girdles. The padded shoulders so popular in the 1930s gave way to the "natural look." Women's clothing took on a lighter appearance as the amount of fabric in their clothing shrank.

To help the home front housewife cope with shortages, several "How To" books appeared on the market. Winifred Rauschenbush, a magazine fashion writer, wrote one of the more interesting books, *How To Dress in Wartime*. Her book was a manual on how to cope with the wartime problems women faced in dressing, including how to make the best out of dressing in slacks, a fashion that, Rauschenbush acknowledged, most men hated with a passion. No less than five chapters in her book are devoted to "slack costumes," for the average figure, the hourglass figure, the wide-shouldered figure, and the slender figure. In addition, Rauschenbush offered advice on how to coordinate slack and skirt costumes for all of the above figures.

In her book, Rauschenbush published a sketch of Paramount Picture's leading lady Claudette Colbert as the "ideal average figure." Ms. Colbert was chosen because her measurements fit the average statistical figures published by the government's Division of Clothing and Textiles (DCC). The DCC measured 15,000 women and concluded that the average American woman ranged in height from five feet two inches to five feet five inches and weighed from a minimum of 116 pounds to a maximum of 134 pounds, depending on frame. Rauschbush wrote: "If your height and weight come within this range, you are an average woman, neither very tall, very short, very heavy, nor very thin. Claudette Colbert has a beautifully proportioned average figure."

Photoplay magazine did its own survey, picking the ten Hollywood stars rated "figure perfect": Betty Grable, Claudette

Colbert, Ginger Rogers, Ann Sheridan, Paulette Goddard, Carol Lombard, Susan Hayward, Loretta Young, Olivia DeHavilland, and Martha Scott. Not making the top ten list, but receiving honorable mention, were Rita Hayworth and Marlene Dietrich.

The ingenuity and length to which women would go to compensate for the loss of "essential" fashion accessories, such as nylon stockings, is illustrated by the use of "leg make-up." Leg make-up was sold to American women as a substitute for nylons. It came in two forms, liquid and solid. The idea was simple. The product was "painted" or rubbed on the leg to simulate stockings. Some products even came with a separate color and fine brush to create the seams that ran up the back of the stockings (for the benefit of today's young women, early nylon stockings were woven with a seam that ran the length of the stocking). The Armand Company of Des Moines, Iowa, made a product called "Stocking Stick," which looked like a piece of brown chalk in the shape of a cube. The instructions were simple: "Wet the legs … Apply stocking stick with a few strokes on front, back, and sides of leg. Then blend the color over the entire surface … at a certain point it begins to thicken to a creamy state … stop stroking at this point, let the make-up dry, and do not touch again." Yuk! It must have felt ghastly, especially on a hot summer night. A final instruction read, "Rubbing of the area above and around the knees to below the skirt line keeps the make-up from coming off on your clothes." Really? "Stocking Stick" came in two shades: "Dawn" and "Sun Valley Tan."

As a child I remember my beautiful Aunt Tessie who had legs like Betty Grable (and a bosom like Dolly Parton) painting her legs with liquid stockings. Sitting on the floor, I was enthralled as she ran the applicator up and down her shapely legs. I still get a little faint when I remember her lifting her skirt and asking, "Are the seams straight?" It was then that I decided the ban on nylon stockings was one of the best things the government did during the war.

Kids suffered no such wardrobe problems. Our standard uniform was simple – a pair of "Buster Brown" shoes (always brown), a shirt, knickers, and knee-high stockings. Knickers are one of those archaic items of dress that go back to Elizabethan England. The dictionary describes knickers as "loose fitting short pants gathered at the knee." The "gathering" was accomplished with a small buckle that loosened or tightened the knicker. The gathering at the knee was one of those strange areas of contention between mother and son. Mothers, for some strange reason, insisted that the knicker be buckled above the knee while boys preferred buckling them below the knee. It was not uncommon to head out for school with your knickers buckled above the knee only to re-buckle them below the knee once safely out of your mother's sight. What mothers never seemed to understand was that the longer knicker was emblematic of the more mature boy, while the shorter knicker (above the knee) was strictly for younger boys who had not yet gained their independence from mom.

Word pundits claim the word knickers is derived from "knickerbockers," a reference to the Dutch settlers of New York City who sported that easily recognized long stockings and short pants look. The word is still used in England and other parts of the British Empire to describe a woman's undergarment, which is another reason they should have been banned in the U.S.

Although popular in the 1920s and 1930s, knickers were still found among the younger generation in the 1940s. Coming of age in wartime America was signaled by receiving your first pair of trousers, usually around the age of ten. The war hastened the end of knickers, thank goodness. They used rubber (elastic bands) and metal (buckles), both essential war materials, making knickers an endangered species, and none to soon for most kids.

* * *

The use of substitute products was widespread throughout the home front. Hundreds of essential war products were replaced by non-rationed alternatives. Butter was replaced by oleomargarine, known simply as "oleo," a by-product made from cottonseed oil. Wood or plastic replaced metal. Adding chicory extended coffee, and milkweed replaced kapok. Kapok! What is kapok you ask? Kapok is the silky fiber found inside the pod that protects the seeds of the Ceiba tree. The bundles of silky fibers found in Ceiba pods entrap air and are impervious to water, making them excellent material for floatation devices like life preservers. The fall of the Malaysian Peninsula to the Japanese in 1942 cut off supplies of kapok to the United States. The seedpod of the milkweed plant, common to the northeastern U.S., is filled with silky fibers that have properties very similar to those of the Ceiba tree. The government mounted a special program asking kids who lived in areas where milkweed grew to harvest the pods and take them to a collection center, usually their school. Among the many things I collected for the war effort, milkweed was high on the list. It was not difficult for one person to find enough milkweed pods growing wild to fill a life preserver, and the thought of some sailor far off at war wearing a life jacket with your very own milkweed inside was thrilling to say the least.

While kapok would help save the lives of many a sailor, it also played a major part in one of the war's early disasters. With the fall of France to Hitler's invading armies, the *Normandie*, France's flagship of luxury ocean liners, was sitting out the conflict at her pier in New York harbor. With the fall of France to the Germans, the *Normandie* was taken over by the U.S. Navy and was being converted for use as a troop transport ship when fire broke out on a lower deck. Before New York fire fighters could bring the fire under control, the *Normandie* filled with water and rolled over on her port side, and died. She was reduced to scrap and sent to the Bethlehem Steel company where her dismembered parts wound up being feed to the plant's open-hearth furnaces. Her demise was not a total loss since her precious scrap metal was reincarnated into new war materials. A Navy investigation attributed the fire to a large pile of kapok stored in the *Normandie*'s hold that had been accidentally ignited by a workman's acetylene torch.

* * *

To many kids the implementation of rationing had little, if any, noticeable effect on their daily lives. The scarcity, and in some cases elimination, of certain commodities impacted our parents far more than us. At least that was the case in my family. While the scarcity of sugar and metal impacted on such kid staples as candy and toys, kids were resilient enough to improvise and "make do" with substitutes. Metal in toys was quickly replaced by non-essential materials such as wood or plastic, and in some cases, by paper. Toy manufacturers were dealt a major blow when the raw materials necessary for production were no longer available. But most recovered quickly.

One example stands out among many. The Daisy Company, manufacturer of every boy's dream, the Daisy Air Rifle (a.k.a. B-B gun), was faced with a crisis of major proportions. Allowed to use up its inventory of metal in the production of air rifles, it could not replace the depleted stock. Metal was the heart of the company's product. To survive, the company retooled its plant to make war-related materials such as shell canisters and special parts for flare pistols. But Daisy did not forget the kids who had supported the company for so many years (Daisy's first air rifle was issued in 1901). The company needed to stay in touch with kids for the day when the war would come to an end and kids would once more want their Daisy air rifles. The company solved its problem by manufacturing two all-wood toy guns, the "Commando" cork-pop rifle and the "Chattermatic," a toy "Tommy" gun.

Upper left: Seifert's grocery store at the corner of Chelsea Avenue and Greenwich Street. *Upper Right*: poster distributed by the Office of War Information, 1942. *Lower left*: Poster published by the Office of War Information, 1943. *Middle right*: Original grocer's store card showing the price in cents and points required to purchase a rationed item. *Lower right*: This building at the corner of Center and Greenwich streets was occupied by Nick Zumas's Sanitary Food Market during the war.

Upper left: War Ration Book One, issued in May 1942. The book was intended for use with certain items when they became available. *Upper right:* Car window stickers denoting the number of gallons of gas the car owner was entitled to. *Middle left*: Ration card for cigarettes. *Middle right*: A ration coupon valued at one point toward the purchase of processed food. *Lower left*: Envelope for holding ration book. *Lower right*: War Ration Book Three, issued in September 1943, intended for clothing rationing that never occurred.

Upper left: A page of ration stamps from War Ration Book Three. These stamps were printed in sheets with pictures of ships, planes, tanks, and guns. They were intended for clothing rationing that never occurred. *Upper right:* A grocer puzzles over the latest ration point schedule. *Middle:* War Ration Book Four, issued in the fall of 1943, was used for processed goods. *Lower:* A tire certificate issued to a lucky citizen for two Grade I passenger tires.

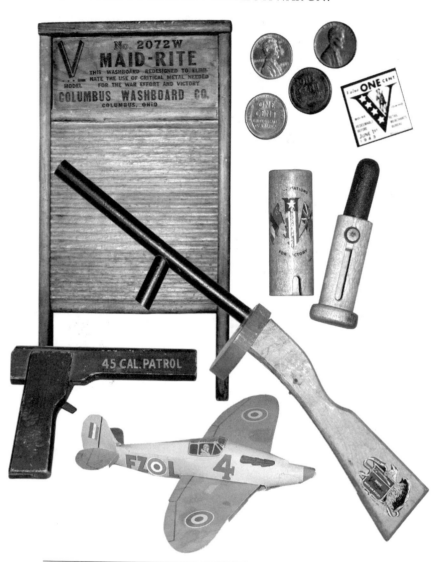

The government banned certain materials used in consumer products. Among the casualties were toys, makeup, pennies, and certain household products. The ribbed surfaces of pre-war washboards were made of zinc-coated steel. The substitute washboard was made entirely of wood, earning the name "Victory Washboard." Copper pennies became a casualty in 1943. The Treasury Department changed to zinc-coated steel. Merchants in Boise, Idaho, issued their own form of penny script called the "Victory Cent." The Treasury Department confiscated the script, ending the venture. Lipstick containers, packaged in a metal tube prior to the war, were replaced with an all-wood tube shown here.The Daisy Company met the metal ban by producing an all-wood "Tommy" gun named the "Chattermatic," and an all-wood pistol with a revolving wooden trigger that "clicked" with every squeeze. Airplanes, pre-cut from a flat sheet of paper, could be assembled into realistic models.

The green dye used to color a pack of Lucky Strike cigarettes contained chromium, a precious metal used in making bronze. A year's supply of the dye was equal to the amount used in 400 tanks. The American Tobacco Company responded by changing the color of their packs to white, giving rise to the slogan *Lucky Strike green has gone to war.* The company pulled the slogan when the public protested, claiming the company was using the war for propaganda purposes. Developed as a substitute for nylon stockings, the "Stocking Stick" was moistened with water then rubbed over the leg, drying into a sticky goop simulating tan-colored stockings. One of the stranger substitutes for metal was a composition made from soybeans. The state of Virginia issued soybean license plates in 1944 in an effort to conserve metal. A waxed cardboard container was designed to replace most metal containers.

Poster promoting Twentieth Century Fox's 1943 movie based on
war correspondent Richard Tregaskis's best-selling book.
An all-star cast portrayed all of the stereotypes that war films favored.

SIX

This is where we came in.

As kids we loved war movies. We couldn't get enough of them. Perhaps it was because our side was made up of Hollywood's greatest heroes, and we always won. Even when we lost, in movies like *Bataan* (MGM, 1943) and *Wake Island* (Paramount, 1942), Hollywood left us feeling that everything was all right. We would return, this time victorious. Hollywood found a way to turn defeat into something noble. The men on Bataan and Wake Island were buying time for General MacArthur and America to marshal its forces and avenge our early defeats. The closing scene in *Wake Island* of Robert Taylor sitting alone in his machine-gun nest blasting away at the charging hoard of Jap soldiers left us more determined than ever. We might have had a temporary setback, but Uncle Sam would come roaring back to ultimate victory.

By 1941, movies had reached their zenith as a popular form of entertainment in the United States. There were more movie theaters in the country than bookstores, and more people went to the movies than read books. At one point during the war, 90 million people were going to the movies every week. The Depression years of the 1930s brought a general malaise to the country except in Hollywood, where moviemakers beguiled us with a fantasy world of singing and dancing and romantic comedy, that ignored the growing menace in Europe and Asia. But that was the way most of us wanted it.

Pearl Harbor brought a crashing end to our naïveté. Just as

Detroit tooled up to start producing tanks, Hollywood tooled up for total war. The tap-dancing musicals of the 1930s were placed on the shelf. But, just as Hollywood had ignored the Depression in the majority of its films of the 1930s, it tended to gloss over the gruesome realities of war. Many of the films were, as Ken Jones and Arthur McClure wrote in *Hollywood at War*, of the "hiss and boo" variety. But "hiss and boo" war movies were what the country needed. The war movies were not an academic exercise in reality. To Americans, the war was black and white. There were good guys and bad guys, and we were the good guys.

As children, our images of war were shaped by the movies. When Hop Harrigan (a radio hero) spoke of a "sneering dirty Nazi," an image of Eric von Stroheim popped into our heads. And who better to play the part of a cruel and ruthless Japanese officer than the great character actor Richard Loo. Invariably, we learned that these Japanese villains were educated in the United States (usually Stanford or Harvard) and wound up biting the hand that fed them – one more example of their treachery. As children, war movies didn't scare us nearly as much as it made us mad – mad at the Nazis and Japanese who fought dirty and laughed while they killed innocent people. Even when the enemy killed our soldiers in the course of battle, there was something sneaky and dirty about the way they did it. Kids from the war years can still see a sneaky Jap sniper hiding high up in a palm tree shooting a young soldier in the back. But in the end, kids knew that the likes of Eric von Stroheim and Richard Loo were no match for John Wayne and Randolph Scott.

* * *

Located in the middle of the block on West Broad Street in Bethlehem is the Boyd movie theater. Built in 1921 as the Kurtz theater, the Boyd became a part of the A.R. Boyd Enterprises of Philadelphia in 1934. The Boyd was typical of the picture palaces that thrived during the heyday of Hollywood films. At least that is the way it seemed to me. Sitting in the theater today it is easy to become lost in a time warp. The only thing missing, besides the grand balcony (now closed to the public), is a good black and white war movie and *Pathé News*.

Unlike most urban theaters that succumbed to blight and competition from suburban multiplex theaters, the Boyd survived thanks to Harold and Joyce Heydt who purchased the theater in 1970 and restored it to its original grandeur. Having survived the economic upheavals of the post-war era, the Boyd soon faced a new crisis. In 1974, city planners in Bethlehem became caught up in the pedestrian-mall craze as an answer to revitalizing the downtown shopping area. The city closed West Broad Street to automobile traffic, including the section where the Boyd was located. The street was converted into an attractive pedestrian park. Thirty years later the city came to the conclusion the idea wasn't working, as local businesses were closing and leaving the area. The city restored the park back to the original street configuration. Throughout the changes and economic upheavals, the Boyd survived and, in some ways, thrived.

Visiting the theater today it seems that little has changed in the intervening years since the war. The Boyd is a large theater consisting of three sections on the main floor and a large balcony that wraps around the rear. Just seeing the balcony today brings back memories of the fun we had during Saturday afternoon matinees. It was a perfect place for launching air attacks on the enemy below, usually with "Good and Plenty" candies as aerial bombs.

A small box office sits at the entrance to the theater flush with the sidewalk. An arcade leads up to six glass doors that open into the carpeted lobby. Inside the lobby are two sets of stairs that lead up to the large balcony. The seating area in the main part of the theater consists of a large center section that seats around 300 people, while to either side, separated by aisles, are the loge areas, each seating 200. On either side of the theater are exit doors marked by signs made of stained glass. During the war years the exit doors were hidden behind heavy drapes to keep out daylight when the doors were opened. In those early days the theater offered a continuous viewing cycle with no start or stop times. Moviegoers could come into the theater at any point during the show and leave at any point they wanted. The phrase "This is where we came in," once commonly used, has long ago passed from the moviegoers' vernacular.

A typical viewing included coming attractions, a newsreel, one or more cartoons, and a "short subject," occasionally a travelogue or humorous skit of slapstick comedy by the Three Stooges or comic Leon Earle. After the feature film ended, the show continued uninterrupted, continuing the cycle starting with Coming Attractions. The whole process "looped" repeatedly.

Admission for the kids' Saturday matinee was ten cents. Trivial by today's standards, a dime was a respectable amount of money during the war. It could purchase a War Savings Stamp. It also purchased two candy bars or five Tootsie Pops, most comic books or a hefty ice cream cone. Newspapers cost anywhere from three cents to a nickel and a loaf of bread cost nine cents (two loaves for 17 cents).

Not every kid had a dime, causing us to resort to anti-social behavior. Sneaking into the movies was one of the more basic skills acquired as a kid. We looked on it as one more example of survival strategy. One kid, usually the one with the least fear, would buy a ticket on pooled money and enter the theater. It was this kid's job to make his way to one of the exits. The Boyd's exit of choice led to an alley behind the theater. Once at the exit door, he would slip behind the drape and open the door just enough to slip a small stick in the opening to prevent the door from closing and locking. Then he would return to his seat in the theater, his job having been completed. Because the shows were continuous without interruption, the theater was always dark.

Unlike today, the exit door was in a small vestibule covered by a heavy curtain to prevent light from disturbing those in the theater when legitimate customers left by way of the exit with the movie still showing. One by one we would open the door just enough to slip inside. The curtain was a blessing because it covered our movements. Once inside the door, we took turns slipping past the curtain and into the theater proper.

Of course, we would time it so that we slipped in at one of the more dramatic moments in the film when the audience's attention was focused on the screen. The only hitch in this dubious activity came if one of the ushers checked the exit to make sure everything was all right. Ushers made regular rounds walking down one aisle and up another, making sure there were no problems, especially on Saturday when the theater was full of kids. Occasionally we were lucky enough that an usher was the older brother of one of the miscreants attempting to sneak in. In this case, the usher would slip a stick in the door and then make sure it was all clear for us to sneak in. I can honestly say that in all the times we were forced to sneak into the Saturday matinee I never remember any of us being caught, so I can't tell you what would have happened to us if we had gotten nabbed, but it would not have been pleasant.

As long as I am in a confessing mood I should tell you of another incident when my brother and I lost our moral compass. This time we were aided by the Secretary of Agriculture, Claude R. Wickard, without whose order of February 1, 1943, we would never have gone astray. Secretary Wickard sent out a notice to retailers that all milk bottles sold after February 1st would carry a one-cent deposit fee. The *Globe-Times* carried a large ad explaining the new policy: "In these war times, it is your patriotic duty to help keep all milk bottles in active use … missing milk bottles cause needless waste of vital war materials and labor."

Can you imagine? Protecting a milk bottle was now your patriotic duty? The one-cent deposit was meant as an incentive to insure that all empty bottles were returned to the store or the dairy.

The Boyd was about a forty-five minute walk from our house. It was probably only a thirty-minute walk if we hadn't fooled around on the way, dodging enemy snipers and tossing imaginary hand grenades at trashcans, pretending they were enemy machine-gun nests. We always used the back alleys that ran behind most every street. Back alleys were our sanctuary where you could duck in and out of small passageways that ran between houses and kick stray tin cans without fear of having someone holler at you.

On that particular Saturday, when my brother and I arrived at the theater, we were shocked to find out that it had raised the admission price for Saturday matinees from ten cents to eleven cents. Since we each had a dime, we were two cents short. Two cents in 1943 was not an inconsequential sum. A penny rise in admission tells you a lot about economics in the 1940s. That penny increase probably translated into five or six dollars for the day's receipts – hardly worth the trouble in today's economy. But during the war, it was a big deal.

Returning home was out of the question. We had to rely on our own resourcefulness. My brother hit on a plan. We quickly backtracked to one of the alleys we had taken to get to the theater. It didn't take long before we spotted our two cents. Setting on the back porch of one of the houses were two unprotected milk bottles. My brother pointed out the target and after briefing me on the plan of attack sent me in to retrieve the two bottles. He would stay back by the garage and keep watch. If someone approached he would signal me with a particular whistle, the one that Tonto used in signaling the Lone Ranger of pending danger. I think it was suppose to sound like a whippoorwill. I was too dumb to know that I would be the one who got into trouble if caught while my brother beat a fast retreat. Such risks, however, go with being the younger brother. With all the stealth of an OSS operative (wartime precursor of the CIA), I made my way slowly along the side of the garage toward the porch and the designated target. I don't want to make it sound too melodramatic, but I snatched two of the bottles and, with a *Shazam!*, beat a rapid retreat back down the alley. Passing my brother at a dead run I handed him one of the bottles. A block later we pulled up to check out our stash. Yep. No doubt about it. They were two genuine penny-deposit bottles.

During the war, milk bottles played an important roll in supporting the war effort. Dairies used their glass bottles as a canvass to carry patriotic slogans. On one side of the bottle was the dairy's logo along with some advertising slogan that reassured those who purchased the milk that it came from only the finest "Golden Guernsey" cows. The milk from Guernsey cows contains a higher butterfat content than from other breeds. Before the days of national obesity and fat consciousness, the higher the butterfat, the better the milk was for kids. The opposite side of the milk bottle contained one of several patriotic slogans: "For Victory Buy War Bonds and Stamps," or "Keep 'em Flying. Buy War Bonds." While milk bottles were worth one cent to the dairy in 1943, "war slogan" bottles today command prices that often exceed one hundred dollars on the collectors' market.

With our booty in hand, we headed straight for the Sanitary Food Market owned by Mr. Zumas. Our plan was to cash in the bottles and beat it back to the theater with the extra two cents. The local grocery store was a lot like the situation with school: the grocer knew you and your parents (and your aunts and uncles and grandparents) and your parents knew them. We had to make sure Mr. Zumas wasn't manning the cash register. He would have looked us over carefully, suspicious of where two kids came up with deposit bottles. Nick, that was his first name, had a couple of older boys working for him on Saturdays stocking shelves, cleaning floors, taking orders over the telephone (they did that sort of thing back then), delivering orders (they also did that), and doing just about anything that needed doing. We entered the store and made our way to the counter where my brother plopped the bottles down. Jimmy, one of the boys working for Nick, saw us coming. He reached into the cash register and took two cents out of the drawer and put the money on the counter. He nodded toward a stack of milk crates at the front of the store filled with empty bottles. My brother picked up the two cents while I shoved the bottles into one of the empty wire slots. We beat a fast retreat out the door and headed back to the theater. Thanks to Secretary Wickard, we were going to the movies.

* * *

When war came, Hollywood jumped into the fracas with both feet, bringing to audiences the right mix of heroic propaganda and a dash of realism. A very small dash, but a dash nonetheless. Hollywood portrayed the war as a life-and-death struggle between democracy and fascism, good and evil, but nearly always in a sanitized form. Death never came quickly to Allied heroes. The rifle shot or grenade explosion seldom produced blood and the victim usually had enough time before he died to make a profound statement. I say "he" because women seldom died as a result of enemy action; instead, their hearts were broken.

Hollywood seldom failed to stereotype its subjects. It was commonplace in many of the war films to include a savvy old veteran, a young, baby-faced kid (who only drank milk), a Jew, a Catholic, a WASP, sometimes a Hispanic or Latino, a hayseed fresh off the farm, a guy from Brooklyn (who loved "dem Bums" and couldn't stop talking about them), and a guy from Texas (invariably called "Tex"). With these stereotypes the picture was sure to be a hit. As naive as this scenario was, it was reassuring to folks on the home front in a time of uncertainty. It seemed even the most dramatic of films had a humorous character and a laughline of some sort. In *Guadalcanal Diary*, a film based on the best-selling book by war correspondent Richard Tregaskis, there was the funny marine played by Robert Rose who kept misplacing his helmet. Whenever the enemy attacked he'd dive behind a tree or stack of oil drums yelling, "Me helmet, me helmet. Where's me helmet?"

To the children of World War II, there was no fantasy, no naiveté. Everything we saw and read was true. To us, John Wayne really was in the Army, and the Air Force, and the Marines, and the Seabees, and the Merchant Marine. Why would we think differently? When we became old enough to enlist, we knew that we would join the same outfit with Wayne and his buddies.

Movies made a deeper impression on us than on our parents and most other adults. Those last few survivors in that gripping movie *Bataan* died as great heroes: Robert Taylor, Lloyd Nolan, George Murphy, Thomas Mitchell, Desi Arnez, Barry Nelson, and Robert Walker – the young kid with peach fuzz on his face and a mom back home that made the "best apple pie in the whole world." The *New York Times* praised the film following its release, writing that MGM "has made a picture about war in true and ugly detail …" The men in *Bataan* not only included a soldier from each ethnic background, it included a black soldier played by Kenneth Spencer. It was Hollywood fantasy, but it made the All-American cast really All-American and it made us feel proud that we were Americans.

The film reinforced our fears and hatred of the Japanese. It had all the stereotypes, good and bad. The Americans stood up and fought like men. The Japanese sneaked around on their bellies with grass and leaves sticking out of their uniforms and helmets. They frequently killed unsuspecting or wounded, defenseless soldiers, using a knife or their bayonets. Slitting throats seemed to be the method of choice for the Japanese. The

Americans killed with a clean shot through the enemy's heart. In the end, the Japs killed American soldiers through stealth. American soldiers would never stoop to use such tactics. They stood up like men.

In 1940 there were 16,000 movie theaters in the country. Between 1941 and 1945 the industry produced 1,700 films of which 550 were classified as war movies. Initially, the government played little or no role in the content of Hollywood's filmmaking. The military often supplied personnel and equipment to filmmakers, but little military or social advice. Then, in the fall of 1942, The Office of War Information (OWI) created its Media Division and began playing a bigger part in the making of movies. OWI began issuing summaries and analyses of feature films. The government was well aware of the effect movies had on the public and their perception of the war.

Prior to 1941, the majority of Americans were opposed to entering a European war. Certain Hollywood studios, owned or run by recent immigrants that had families under Nazi occupation, began making anti-Fascist films to influence public opinion. Movies like *Confessions of a Nazi Spy* (Warner Brothers, 1939) starring Edward G. Robinson, and *The Mortal Storm* (MGM, 1940) with an all-star cast headed by Jimmy Stewart and Robert Young.

Confessions of a Nazi Spy was the first anti-Nazi film produced by an American film studio. It brought strong protests from Nazi diplomats in America and American anti-war protesters who believed the film was meant to stir up pro-war sentiment against Germany. They were right. *The Mortal Storm* was a chilling film that showed the effect of Nazism on a German family headed by a kindly university professor (played by Frank Morgan, the wizard in *The Wizard of Oz*). The professor's two sons (Robert Stack and William Orr) join the Nazi party only to see their father arrested and sent to a concentration camp for his democratic beliefs. The professor's daughter (Margaret Sullavan) falls in love with one of her father's students and close family friend, played by Jimmy Stewart. Sullavan attempts to flee Germany with Stewart by skiing down the mountain slopes toward Switzerland and freedom. Chased by a Nazi ski patrol, the two lovers get within a few hundred feet of the border when one of the Nazi snipers wounds Sullavan. Unable to leave his lover behind, the two are murdered within feet of the Swiss border and freedom. The film was depressing to most Americans, but it nonetheless strengthened anti-Nazi sentiment throughout the country. Hitler reacted angrily to the film by banning all of MGM's movies throughout Germany and her occupied territories.

* * *

War movies were made for adults, not kids, and while kids enjoyed certain war movies, our real passion was for the Saturday matinees and the ever-popular "serials." Serials were actually a series of movie chapters shown on successive Saturdays over a period of several weeks. A complete serial, in most cases, consisted of fifteen chapters. Each Saturday the theater would show one of the chapters until the serial was completed. For twenty minutes the hero and heroine faced a series of incredible adventures involving all sorts of fantastic fight scenes with evil criminals intent on taking over the world (and the beautiful heroine in the process). Serial plots were invariably the same whether they took place in outer space (*Flash Gordon*), out West (*Zorro's Black Whip*), in the Orient (*Drums of Fu Manchu*), in Canada (*King of the Royal Mounted*), in the air (*Sky Raiders*), in the city (*Batman*), or in the Jungle (*Jungle Queen*). Each chapter ended with the same high drama. For example, the unconscious hero (or heroine) lies trapped in a blazing warehouse surrounded by barrels of TNT (or in a runaway wagon about to go over a cliff). Just as the flames begin licking up the side of a barrel that is marked in large bold letters "Danger – TNT," the words "Don't miss next week's thrilling episode!" are emblazoned across the screen. Next week the hero (or heroine) wakes up just in the nick of time to flee the burning building (or jump from the wagon as it plummets over the edge of the cliff).

There were several serials that dealt with the war, always involving spies determined to steal a secret formula that would win the war for the Axis powers. Perhaps the best serial was *Secret Agent X-9*, starring a young and upcoming Lloyd Bridges and that wonderfully sinister actor, Keye Luke. Luke made a career scaring the bejeepers out of kids (and a few adults) as the sneaky, hissing, Jap bad guy. One of the most memorable lines in my cerebral file cabinet is delivered by Keye Luke dressed as a Jap colonel as he greets an American pilot taken prisoner. Pausing to light a cigarette, Luke smiles sinisterly and says, "You surprised I speak your language, Yankee?"

* * *

To children, the war movies were educational in many ways. We learned from films such as *Action in the North Atlantic* that the Merchant Marine service was an important part of the war effort. Most of us had never heard of the Merchant Marine let alone understood the important role it played. We also learned about the Navy's Construction Battalion, known as the "Seabees" (CBs), through films like *The Fighting Seabees*. As with the Merchant Marine, the Seabees were a branch of service unknown to most Americans. Their motto, "Can Do," became one of the fighting slogans of the home front. No task was too big or too difficult to accomplish. When asked if it could be done, the answer was invariably, "Can Do!" The phrase became a part of our language.

World War II, in fact, gave rise to a whole vocabulary of new words and phrases, and the movies were in the forefront of exposing both adults and kids to this new jargon. Just as we

Top left: Advertisement from the *Globe-Times* for Walt Disney's popular film *Dumbo*, Christmas 1941. *Top right*: Still picture from MGM's 1943 movie *Bataan*. *Below left*: Still picture from MGM's 1939 anti-Nazi film *The Mortal Storm*. *Below right*: Advertisement promoting Paramount Pictures' stirring 1942 war film *Wake Island*. Included in the ad is a facsimile letter by President Roosevelt citing the heroic defenders.

Sheet music for the stirring song "*Any Bonds Today?*" Written by Irving Berlin, the song was copyrighted in 1941 by Henry Morgenthau, Jr., Secretary of the Treasury, and sung at hundreds of War Bond rallies across the nation. It was originally adopted as the theme song of the National Defense Savings Program. Warner Brothers produced a popular cartoon featuring Bugs Bunny singing the song as a promotion selling war stamps and bonds in movie theaters.

SEVEN

Any Bonds Today?

 On those mornings when I flew over Kunsman's field, my destination was Hamilton Elementary School, located a mile from my house. Hamilton was typical of many neighborhood schools built in the 1920s and 1930s. A modest two-story brick structure, it was built to accommodate single classes of grades one through six. The era of consolidated school districts with several classrooms for each grade was still in the future. At Hamilton, a single class of thirty students spent six years together as it moved from grades one through six with teachers and a principal who knew you and, in most instances, knew your family. In fact, it was not unusual to find a teacher who taught your own parents or went to school with them. This personal relationship between teacher and family was a two-edged sword. Because many of the teachers and the principal knew your parents, it gave them a psychological advantage over you and your behavior. Poor performance or disruptive behavior would reach your parents quickly and "remedial" steps were swift and effective. It was a time in the educational system when teachers meted out discipline and parents did not object. In fact, double jeopardy was the rule of the day. Joanne Cacciola remembers her war days as a student at Hamilton: "We were taught to respect our teachers and they did no wrong. I made sure I behaved and didn't get in trouble, 'cause if I did, I'd be in double trouble when I got home."

I still have vivid memories of standing at attention in the

principal's office, legs trembling beneath me as our principal, Mr. Rinker, sat staring at me for several minutes. The day before, I had made one of my more stupid blunders. After school had let out for the day, I was standing on the sidewalk out front fooling around with two of my classmates when I looked up at the window of the principal's office on the second floor. In a moment that can only be described as temporary insanity, I began shouting, "Mr. Rinker is a stinker!" After a few minutes all three of us took off running as fast as we could. The next morning, when I was summoned to the office, Mr. Rinker proceeded to remind me that he knew my mother and father. My mother, he said, was a good mother who tried to raise her children to be polite and well mannered. How ashamed she would be to learn of my misbehavior. By the time he finished his upbraiding I had terrible visions of my mother sitting at the kitchen table, her head buried in her hands, sobbing uncontrollably. Never again could she appear in public without feeling the shame I had brought on her by my bad behavior. She would henceforth have to wear the letters "BB" prominently displayed on her dress letting the whole world know that she was the mother of a "Bad Boy." Mr. Rinker was a master at mind games. Such psychology was sufficient to bring about deep feelings of guilt and remorse along with a blood-oath that such behavior would never, ever happen again.

Unfortunately, the life of a junior warrior in times of war often resulted in situations that made it necessary to set aside blood-oaths if the country was to be saved from its Axis enemies. Dive-bombing female classmates during recess was essential to the war effort even if it did result in chastisement by the principal. At times, our school was converted into a Stalag and our principal into an Obergruppenfuhrer, but it was all part of war.

My second-grade teacher was Mrs. Elda Oestreicher, a matronly woman who was endowed with all of the good qualities a teacher should have when entrusted with the minds of other people's children. She was an imposing woman who demanded, and received, strict attention at all times. Among her many skills was dentistry. Although lacking a DDS degree, she nonetheless practiced the craft routinely. She was so well known for her dental expertise that the other teachers used her as a referral service. Any student who was foolish enough to get caught wiggling a loose tooth with their tongue instantly fell under her care. Once spotted, class would come to a halt and the unlucky victim would be summoned to the front of the room where he (or she) would undergo an "extraction," without the benefit of Novocain. Carefully tucked in the opening between the buttons of her bodice was a frilly lavender-scented handkerchief that was the dread of every loose-toothed kid in school. To this day the smell of lavender sends a chill up my spine.

Instructed to stand straight with arms behind your back and mouth wide open, the dreaded hanky would clutch the wiggly tooth. Fortunately, Mrs. O's grip was sure, and her skill as an extraction specialist was beyond reproach. A quick twist followed by a yank and it was over, tooth and jaw separated. Mrs. O would slip open one of her desk drawers and drop the liberated tooth into a jar. At least that is what it sounded like – a tinkly clink. Whatever happened to all those teeth is a mystery, but they probably wound up serving the war effort in some way – every-thing else did, why not children's teeth? Bing Van Nuys, another classmate, remembers the time *he* was caught wiggling a loose tooth. "I was called to the front of the class where Mrs. O pulled out the loose tooth with her handkerchief. My parents were not too thrilled," Bing wrote. "Today, it would be grounds for a lawsuit and criminal charges."

* * *

Among the more important school activities was the weekly ritual of purchasing War Stamps. Once a week kids formed a line ending at the teacher's desk. Squeezed between thumb and forefinger was a silver dime. Dimes were the most common denomination of stamps, although there was always one kid who showed up with a quarter, waving it in your face to let you know how well off he was.

We each took our turn stepping up to the desk and plunking down our dime. In return we received a small carmine-colored postage stamp, similar to a postage stamp, bearing the image of a minuteman standing ready to defend his country. Now it was our turn to help defend it from the likes of Hitler and his gang. Our sacrifice was not trivial. During the war, candy bars cost five cents (and were twice the size of today's bars), and bubble gum was a penny. Admission to the Saturday matinee at the Boyd was ten cents (until late in the war when the price jumped to eleven cents). But since rationing limited things like sugar and cocoa, there were not that many candy bars or bubble gum to go around. Still, ten cents could buy a whole lot more then than it can today.

Each kid had a small stamp album that fit inside his lunch pail. Inside the albums were carefully marked boxes where the newly purchased stamps were pasted. Beneath each box was a running total of the amount of money your book was worth. Beginning with ten cents, the total ran for several pages, ending with that special box designating $18.70. Buying a stamp a week, it took twenty-seven weeks to fill an album. The album, along with a nickel (a bond cost $18.75), was exchanged for a $25.00 United States War Bond.

Bonds were truly beautiful objects to behold! Printed on the same paper used for currency, the early war bonds measured 8 inches square and were bordered with beautiful engraving that resembled a spider's web. Each bond carried a "Table of Redemption Values" right on the front so you could see just how much interest accumulated every six months. In ten years, your investment of $18.75 returned $25.00. Not a great deal as far as investments went, but the really important fact was that you were actually purchasing war materiel with each stamp.

Posted on the bulletin board outside one of the classrooms was a large colorful poster that said, "Do Your Part To Help Win the War – Buy More War Savings Stamps." The poster was one of hundreds produced by the government to inform and inspire people during the war. Many of the posters had messages that quickly became part of our wartime language. Messages like: "Back the Attack," or "Loose Lips Sink Ships," and, of course, "Remember Pearl Harbor."

The poster was a large checkerboard. In each of the odd numbered boxes were pictures of an essential war item such as a helmet or a rifle. In the even numbered boxes were statements telling how many War Savings Stamps were needed to purchase the particular item in the adjoining box. This was another way kids were encouraged to buy war stamps. By actually seeing what a stamp or bond would buy, we could relate to where our money was going.

On the back of the poster was a set of suggestions to the teacher on how to use the chart in promoting a school savings program and, at the same time, have it be an effective learning tool. For example, the guide suggests the teacher ask her students questions such as, "If three 10-cent stamps will pay for 2 sandbags, how much does 1 sandbag cost?" That was a pretty simple question. But there were difficult ones too: "A life boat picked up 8 men wearing self-inflating life belts. What was the combined cost of the float and gas for the life belts, in 10-cent stamps?" The solution to these questions could be found on the poster: "Two 10-cent stamps will pay for gas for one self-inflating life belt," and "ten $18.75 bonds will pay for one life float." The answer: the gas for eight belts costs $1.60 (2x10x8), and the life float cost $187.50 (10 x 18.75).

We not only learned the cost of a rubber life float (raft), we also learned that such a float was meant to accommodate eight men. We learned that eleven 25-cent War Savings Stamps would buy a soldier's helmet, while three 10-cent War Savings Stamps would pay for two pairs of socks. A 25-cent War Savings Stamp paid for one month's feed for one carrier pigeon. The same stamp would buy an entire clip of ammunition for the army's Garand rifle. We also learned that the Garand rifle was self-loading and could fire 60 shots a minute up to an effective range of 3,500 yards. This was essential information that every red-blooded American boy needed to know. Buying ammunition for a Garand rifle was heady stuff for most boys, while girls were more inclined to feed carrier pigeons. After all, as one girl pointed out, "You can't pet a rifle or cuddle it like you can a fluffy carrier pigeon," all of which goes to show how ignorant girls were about the Garand rifle.

Buying War Savings Stamps every week through school was serious business. A few miles to the north of Bethlehem is the neighboring town of Nazareth, another of the biblical place-names that are found throughout the Lehigh Valley. During the 1943–44 school year, the students at Nazareth High School purchased the incredible sum of $60,670 in War Bonds and $675.10 in War Stamps. The major part of these sales occurred during the school's "Buy-A-Plane" campaign. The object of the bond drive was to raise enough money through the sale of bonds and stamps to purchase a fighter plane for the Army Air Corps. The money raised fell short of buying an actual plane, but for their efforts, the U.S. Army had the name of the high school painted on the instrument panel of a Fairchild PT-19 trainer airplane where an army pilot was sure to see it during his training. The student body was justifiably proud of their patriotic effort.

According to government figures released after the war, in 1944 alone, schools financed 2,900 airplanes, 33,000 jeeps, 11,600 amphibious jeeps, and 11,690 parachutes, all through the purchase of War Bonds and Stamps. These are impressive numbers even when stacked up against the total investment in

War Bonds made by our parents. The total of all "E" bonds (smallest denomination bonds) sold between May 1941 and June 1945 was $36 billion. Of this grand total, kids accounted for just over $1 billion through their schools, or an average of $20.00 per kid, per year. It was an impressive figure when one considers that the average income for a family at the start of the war was only $2,000 per year.

Prior to Pearl Harbor, War Savings Bonds were called Defense Savings Bonds. President Roosevelt's Secretary of the Treasury, Henry Morgenthau, launched a campaign beginning in 1940 to get Americans to buy Defense Bonds. Morgenthau's interest was not to raise money to support the government's costly military buildup, but to get the American people to feel they had a stake in the government and its support for our European Allies, and for the war that Morgenthau and others felt was coming. By buying bonds, Americans were loaning their government money, which was then used to support war mobilization. After Pearl Harbor, Americans were virtually 100 percent united behind the war effort. Morgenthau rightly pointed out that millions of Americans were asking, "What can we do to help?" Buying bonds, Morgenthau said, was one way every American could help. Between November 30, 1942, and December 8, 1945, the War Finance Committee, the agency responsible for the War Savings Bond program, held eight bond drives. Each drive lasted approximately three weeks, and each drive exceeded its goal. In all, the eight loan drives raised a little over $155 billion from the sale of bonds. The grand total for all bond sales of all types during the war came to just over $190 billion, which equaled half of the total cost of the war.

As with other programs of home front activity, the War Advertising Council played a major role in promoting bond sales at no cost to the government. Private businesses supplied the personnel and advertising space in promoting sales primarily in magazines and newspapers, but radio was not far behind in giving free airtime to promote sales. The mellifluous voice of Hollywood's Orson Welles appealed to us over the radio: "Send Uncle Sam a dime to help win this war ... and when victory comes, you'll have war bonds in your pockets instead of Axis bonds on your wrists."

The government invested heavily in large, colorful posters to get the message across to the public. Posters appeared everywhere – in post offices, grocery and department stores, small shop windows, factory locker rooms, executive office buildings, and in schools. Posters depicting a soldier hugging a young girl with tears in her eyes: "We can't all go ... but we can all help!" the message on the poster read. A factory worker standing alongside a soldier with the message: "Every $3.00 you put into War Bonds buys 144 bullets for his rifle." Some posters appealed to our collective guilt, like the poster of a young woman holding a baby. She is looking directly at us and says: "I gave a man! Will you give at least 10% of your pay in War Bonds?" How could we refuse?

Not all posters were of a serious nature. Some relied on humor to sell their messages, like the poster with cartoon depictions of Hitler, Goering and Goebbels. The poster is a play on words. "Bunds" were pro-German organizations formed in the United States by German-American citizens prior to the war. The Bunds supported Germany's new prosperity under Hitler. When Germany declared war on the U.S., the Bunds disbanded, its members supporting the Allied cause. In the poster, Hitler appears to be excited as he says, "It is goot to hear Americans are now pudding 10% of der pay into Bunds!" Goebbels whispers into Goering's ear, "Herman, you tell him it iss BONDS – not BUNDS!"

Just as we gave at school, our mothers and fathers gave at work. The government launched a major plan to get workers to give 10 percent of their wages to war bonds every payday through a payroll deduction plan. Rather than get people to invest in bonds by scaring them with the horrors of fascism, the government appealed to their economic well-being. The government's pamphlet writers pointed out that "The completion of the [10%] plan will help everybody after the war – business – labor – and the government. It will help ensure jobs for workers in making peacetime goods again. It will provide millions of customers with the money to buy these goods." The pamphlet went on to ask and answer the question, why: "Because – the income of the United States is the highest in history – $120 billion for 1942. Purses are full! Goods are scarce … and getting scarcer every day. In spite of price ceilings, inflation will burst through unless at least 12 billion dollars is taken from national income and invested in War Bonds."

This extraordinary appeal seems to run counter to logic, and yet it worked. An appeal was made to workers on the basis of their own self-interest, not just the government's need for money to support the war. In fact, the government acknowledged that the 10 percent plan would bring the government more money than it needed to prosecute the war. It wrote: "Why 10%? Because the government wants a 'cushion' to prevent the hard times that usually follow every war." It went on to point out, "Think what 12 billion dollars a year saved now by millions of people … can buy when the war ends!" The government candidly told us, "We want to make every citizen of this country take a bigger interest in his government … by giving him a stake in that government!" This candidness was the first instance of truth in borrowing.

The payroll deduction plan proved to be good but not exceptional. During the period from April 1942 (the start of the plan) to April 1945, a total of $16 billion was deducted from workers' salaries for War Bonds through the payroll deduction plan. This amounted to an average of $640 per worker for the three-year period the plan was in effect, or just over $200 a year.

The payroll deduction plan did remove a large amount of

money from circulation, which helped to hold down inflation. The government used special "War Loan" drives to raise additional money outside the workplace. And it did it without spending a dime. Private corporations picked up the tab, which helped to boost Uncle Sam's profit margin. Radio stations used their top stars and donated free airtime for commercials urging listeners to support the war effort through their bond purchases. Kate Smith, who created a second national anthem with her stirring rendition of Irving Berlin's God Bless America, raised $40 million in a one-day radiothon in the fall of 1943.

The bond drives were grueling work and occasionally dangerous. On January 16, 1942, just one month after the attack on Pearl Harbor, one of the movie industry's biggest stars, Carol Lombard, was killed in a plane crash while returning home from a bond rally where she helped sell over 2 million dollars in bonds. Lombard was married to one of the screen's leading male actors, Clark Gable. Gable was devastated by Lombard's death and went into seclusion. When he emerged several months later, he enlisted in the Army Air Corps and was assigned to the 351st Bomb Group. In October 1943, Gable was assigned to the Eighth Air Force, based in England. "What I want," Gable said, "is to be a machine gunner on an airplane." He almost got his wish. Too old to fly combat missions, he flew operational missions over Europe, shooting film for training purposes. His job completed, he was allowed to resign with the rank of major on June 12, 1944, six days after the D-Day invasion of Europe. Stars like Gable were far more valuable to the war effort on the home front than on the battlefront.

Hollywood not only used its stars to help sell bonds, it used its own house – the movie theater. In 1942, virtually all movie theaters sold stamps and bonds on the premises. They also took up collections for the Red Cross and Community Chest from its patrons, who were psychologically primed after watching a war movie filled with heroism and sacrifice. One of the more effective methods used to get people to donate involved special promotional films using actors and actresses. Hollywood's most popular stars would appear on screen acting out a skit discussing patriotism and the need for sacrifice. The action would stop and the featured star would "walk up" to the audience and make a pitch to buy bonds. In one such skit, Tyrone Power interrupts a film shoot and turns to the audience and says: "For the love of our country and for the sake of our boys who are fighting for you, please don't leave this theater without buying your share of War Bonds and Stamps. Thank you." Most people couldn't say no.

In perhaps their biggest effort of the war, the theater industry undertook a special bond campaign to raise $130 million to build an aircraft carrier named *Shangri-La*. Shangri-La was the name President Roosevelt gave to his mountain retreat located in the Catoctan Mountains near present-day Thurmont, Maryland. Roosevelt took the name from a popular movie titled *Lost Horizon*. In the movie, Shangri-La was a mythical paradise located somewhere in the Himalayan Mountains. Roosevelt's retreat was later renamed "Camp David" by President Eisenhower, after his grandson, David Eisenhower, and continues to serve as a presidential mountain retreat.

In 1942, less than one year into the war, the Army Air Corps launched a spectacular raid on Tokyo using B-25 medium range bombers launched from the aircraft carrier USS *Hornet*. The raid became known as "The Doolittle Raid," after the bomb group's commanding officer, Colonel Jimmy Doolittle. Everyone was taken by surprise, especially the Japanese. Americans were elated.

No one believed a medium range bomber like the B-25 could be launched from an aircraft carrier. The runway was not long enough for a safe takeoff. Under the careful eye of Doolittle, his men practiced for several weeks on land until every pilot could successfully make the short takeoff required by the flight deck of the *Hornet*. Being able to land a B-25 on a carrier deck was unnecessary. After dropping their bombs on Tokyo, the planes continued heading west to Mainland China where several made forced landings.

The Doolittle Raid was a great morale builder during the darkest days of the war. While the raid had little effect on Japan's production effort, it had a major psychological effect on the Japanese people, and on the American people. It showed the Japanese they were vulnerable in their own homeland, while it gave the American people a tremendous lift knowing we were able to take the war to the Japanese homeland and gain a small measure of revenge for Pearl Harbor. Launching the raid from an aircraft carrier was a closely kept secret because neither the Japanese nor American people believed it could be done. The Japanese were convinced the planes had to be launched from a secret airstrip somewhere in China.

After the raid, President Roosevelt held a press conference and, when asked where the planes took off from, broke into a broad smile, telling the reporters, "Shangri-La," referring to the mythical place in the Himalayan Mountains featured in the movie *Lost Horizon*. Now movie theaters all across America would sell war stamps and bonds to build an aircraft carrier named the USS *Shangri-La*.

The campaign ran the entire month of July 1942. The goal was aimed at getting a dollar from every man, woman, and child in the country (130 million). Slogans like "The showman's 'Bucket Brigade' will build the Shangri-La!" and "Everybody in America has a dollar for Uncle Sam!" Promotional materials were sent to 16,000 theaters, urging owners to hold special "Kid's Matinees." Because, as the brochure accompanying the promotional material pointed out, "Kids are naturals for this! ... And if they get the romantic story of the great aircraft carrier, which will be built with THEIR dimes – they'll give them. Run a special Kiddie matinee – You'll get results!"

Just what funds were actually raised and whether any of the money was actually earmarked for carrier construction is unclear, but on January 15, 1943, construction began on the *Shangri-La* at the Norfolk Navy Yard. Mrs. Jimmy Doolittle christened the ship on February 24, 1944. The carrier eventually made its way to the Pacific where its planes supported the Tenth Army in the fight to capture the Japanese island of Okinawa. In May 1945, the *Shangri-La* became the flagship of the 2nd Carrier Task Force under the command of Vice Admiral John S. McCain. (His son John S. McCain, Jr. was also an admiral – the only father-son to become full admirals in U.S. history. His grandson John McCain III, a senator from Arizona and a Navy pilot and POW, served in Vietnam).

The ship was decommissioned in 1971 and placed in the Atlantic Reserve Fleet until August 1982 when she was disposed of by the Marine Administration. She was cut into pieces and sold as scrap.

* * *

Movie theaters in the 1940s regularly included one or more cartoons as part of its matinee showings. One of the more inspirational cartoons featured the popular Warner Brothers' rabbit, Bugs Bunny. Bugs, wearing a helmet and carrying a rifle, marched across the silver screen singing one of Irving Berlin's patriotic songs:

> Any bonds today?
> Bonds of freedom that's what I'm selling –
> Any bonds today?
> Scrape up the most you can –
> Here comes the freedom man,
> Asking you to buy a share of freedom today!"*

Selling war bonds was a big business and nearly every business, large or small, helped out in some way. The award for the most unusual "place of business" selling bonds, however, has to go to the Northhampton County Prison (the city of Bethlehem falls within Northhampton County). Warden Irvin Glackenbach issued a press release proudly announcing that the inmates under his care purchased $500 in War Bonds and contributed $50 in cash to the American Red Cross. There is no doubt the Second World War was a war that saw every man, woman, and child join the effort to make the world safe for democracy – even those who were behind bars.

SOURCES

The *Bethlehem Globe Times*, December 1941 – December 1942.

Jack Goodman, ed., *While You Were Gone. A Report on Wartime Life in the United States* (New York: Simon & Schuster, 1946).

Richard R. Lingeman, *Don't You Know There's a War On? The American Home Front 1941-1945.* (New York: G. P. Putnam's Sons, 1970).

Geoffrey Perrett, *Days of Sadness, Years of Triumph. The American People 1939-1945* (Baltimore, MD. Penguin Books, Inc., 1974).

* Words and music by Irving Berlin, copyright by Henry Morgenthau, Jr., Secretary of the Treasury, Washington, D.C.

Top left: $25 War Savings Bond, 1942. *Top right*: War Savings Stamps in denominations from 10 cents to $5.00. *Right*: Patriotic stamp book designed for children. *Below*: A stamp book with 10-cent stamps.

THIS IS YOUR Ten-Cent Defense Stamp Album. Fill it with 187 Ten-Cent Defense Stamps. Add 5c in coin, and it will have a value of $18.75. Exchange it at the post office for a Defense Savings Bond which, after 10 years, will be worth $25. Then start filling another Defense Stamp Album.

Defense Stamps are sold in five denominations—10c, 25c, 50c, $1, and $5. With your first purchase of any Defense Stamp, you are entitled to receive, free of charge, an Album for mounting that kind of Stamp. Mount none but 10c Defense Stamps in this Album. Be sure to affix Stamps securely.

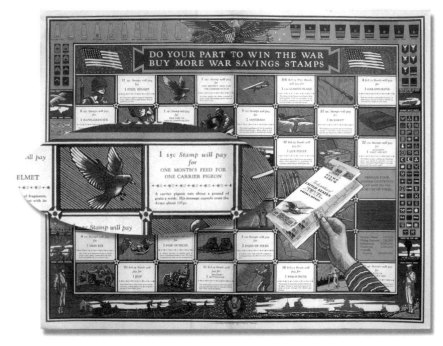

Above: A 1943 government poster in the form of a checkerboard showing school students what their War Stamps would purchase. Inset shows that one 25-cent stamp will buy one month's feed for a carrier pigeon. *Below left*: Comic book heroes join together to simulate the raising of the American flag on Iwo Jima (1945). *Below right*: Government poster promoting War Bonds, using the popular slogan *"Keep him flying"* (1943).

Top left: Match book. *Top right*: Armband worn by persons selling War Stamps at school. *Middle left*: Coaster telling how many bullets a 25-cent stamp will buy. *Middle right*: Government poster using humor and ridicule to promote War Bonds. *Bottom*: Patriotic envelope promoting War Bonds.

One of a series of boys' adventure stories by former Royal Air Force pilot
R. Sidney Bowen. Bowen also wrote a popular series featuring
an American hero named Dave Dawson.

EIGHT

Books are bullets in the war against fascism.

Next to listening to the radio and going to the movies, books were an important source of information for kids. In Bethlehem there are two major sources of books, the public library and the Moravian Book Shop. The Moravian Book Shop is owned and operated by the Moravian Church. The profits from sales go toward supporting the Moravian Ministerial Pension Fund. The Moravians claim the Book Shop, founded in 1745, is the oldest bookstore in continuous operation in the country.

The book store was a favorite of my grandmother, and not a birthday or Christmas went by that I did not receive a book from the Moravian Book Shop. Nowadays most kids do not consider books much of a birthday or Christmas present, but sixty years ago books were welcomed gifts. The store was heavily stocked with the traditional classics like *King Arthur, Treasure Island, Gulliver's Travels, Penrod* (with Duke, "his wistful dog"), and the more contemporary adventure series like *The Hardy Boys, Tom Swift,* and *Buddy.* The rich illustrations of N.C. Wyeth in *The Boy's King Arthur* captured my imagination. The very image of Wyeth's Sir Lancelot du Lake or Arthur and Mordred locked in mortal combat widened the eyes of many a boy who gazed upon it. These and numerous other classics were always in stock at the Moravian Book Shop.

Today the store has expanded its inventory well beyond books to include a variety of whimsies and gimcracks. It continues to be the finest bookstore in the area, carrying quality titles in a broad range of subjects – including the classics that educated an earlier generation.

The Bethlehem Public Library used the war to promote their reading program for children using a clever device. Posted on the wall near the front desk was a large chart with the names of kids who "enlisted" in the library's reading program. Running across the top of the chart were military ranks ranging from private to general. For each book read (checked out and returned) you received points advancing you in military rank – one book for private, two books for corporal, and so forth up through to general. To become a general you had to read somewhere around 20 or 25 books; I can't remember how many but it really doesn't matter because I never reached the rank of general. Each visit to the library included a close study of the chart to see where you stood among your peers in the competition to become a general.

Kids learned a great deal about the war from adventure books written by a few prolific writers who supplied us with dozens of exciting war stories. As with other areas of consumer products, wartime restrictions on publishing had no noticeable effect on kids. There was an ample supply of comic books and plenty of war books to satisfy our appetites for adventure. Among the heroes for boys were Dave Dawson, Lucky Terrell, Red Randall, and Dick Donnelly. Girls' wartime heroines included Norma Kent (of the WACS), Sally Scott (of the WAVES), and Mary Mason (of the Ferry Command). Interestingly, all of the "girl" stories were written by men. The storybook heroes and heroines, together with their radio cousins Captain Midnight, Hop Harrigan, Terry Lee and Little Orphan Annie, were a formidable force for good in the daily struggle against the Axis powers.

For the duration of the war I put aside Penrod and Arthur and took up with the likes of Dave Dawson. The most prolific author of children's war stories was R. Sidney Bowen, the creator of Dave Dawson and his pal, Freddy Farmer. Bowen was a veteran of World War I, when he flew for the Royal Flying Corps. After the war he became a newspaper journalist, test pilot, and editor of an aviation magazine before writing war adventure stories. Between 1941 and 1946, Bowen wrote fifteen books in his Dave Dawson series that saw Dave and Freddie fight their way from Dunkirk through Libya, Singapore, Guadalcanal, Casablanca, and Truk (all book titles). The pair also fought in the RAF (Royal Air Force), alongside the Russians on the Russian Front, in China with General Chennault and his Flying Tigers, on the high seas with the Pacific Fleet, and on Convoy Patrol (again, all book titles).

Dave Dawson is a young American who begins his war adventures in 1940. By the way, did you notice that most of these hero-types had first and last names all beginning with the same letter of the alphabet? – Dick Donnelly, Red Randall, Mary Mason and Sally Scott. To get back to Dave Dawson – Dave is visiting Paris at the time the Germans invade France. As the German army advances, pushing the Brits to the English Channel at a place called Dunkirk, Dave escapes Paris and makes his way to Dunkirk where he meets up with Freddie Farmer, an Englishman trapped with the British forces (*Dave Dawson at Dunkirk*). The two escape and make their way to England where Dave and Freddie join together, undertaking a series of missions that take them through every campaign in the Eastern Theater of the war.

Sydney Bowen's style of writing is exceptionally good and his stories are quite thrilling. Bowen leans heavily on intelligence work involving agents from both sides of the war. In some ways Dave Dawson is the young adult's James Bond. In one especially exciting episode, from *Dave Dawson with the Air Corps*, Dave and Freddie are given the daring assignment of stopping the notorious Nazi agent code-named "Seven-Eleven." Seven-Eleven's mission is to blow up the Panama Canal. I won't give away the ending to this thriller (you might guess the ending anyway), but to this day I can't go into a 7-11 store without wondering if it isn't linked in some way to Germany's great spy. If hundreds of Nazi war criminals were able to make their way to Argentina (and some to Northern Virginia!) at the end of the war, why couldn't Germany's greatest spy make his way to the U.S. and open up a chain of convenience stores as a cover for his new persona?

* * *

With the coming of war, the book industry was faced with good news–bad news. The bad news was that paper shortages forced publishers to cut back on the number of titles and to squeeze more type onto every page by narrowing the borders. The good news was that book sales increased to all-time record highs. Writers faced a similar good news–bad news scenario. The good news was people were buying more books than ever. The bad news was publishers were only accepting the works of well established authors. The number of titles published in 1945 (5,600) was half the number published in 1941 (11,000).

In the first year of the war, libraries showed a 15 percent increase in books borrowed. Unlike current trends, non-fiction outsold fiction by a wide margin. The public's appetite for war-related books, especially "eye-witness" accounts of the type written by war correspondents, topped the list. Books like *Guadalcanal Diary* (Richard Tregaskis) and *They Were Expendable* (William L. White) were instant best-sellers (both were made into highly successful films). The non-fiction best-seller in 1941 was *Berlin Diary*, an eyewitness account of Germany under the Nazis, written by William L. Shirer, Berlin chief correspondent for CBS. For the next four years books about the war would dominate the non-fiction best-seller list. *See Here Private Hargrove* (Marion Hargrove) in 1942, *Under Cover* (John Roy Carlson) and *One*

World (Wendell Wilkie) in 1943, *Brave Men* (Ernie Pyle) and *I Never Left Home* (Bob Hope) in 1944, and *Brave Men* again in 1945. These and similar books were the vehicle through which most Americans learned about the war and their countrymen fighting it. With best-sellers showing larger sales than ever, one book stood out from all the rest: *One World* by Wendell Wilkie. Wilkie, the defeated Republican candidate for president in 1940, toured the world on a goodwill mission in 1943 at the behest of President Roosevelt. On his return, Wilkie wrote his view of the coming peace, pointing out that the post-war world would be one world geographically and politically. Wilkie's book broke every sales record in the country. It sold 200,000 copies in the first 72 hours following its release. By the end of the year, an unprecedented 2 million copies had sold – at a time when the population of the country was 132 million, less than half of what it is today.

Radio was children's number one source of war information through afternoon and evening adventure serials, with movies second, comic books and children's books a close third. William M. Tuttle, Jr., in his interesting study on children and World War II (*Daddy's Gone to War*), writes there were 150 different comic books that sold 20 million copies each and every month during the war. Tuttle writes that the Captain Marvel Club (who, by the way, supported Wilkie's view of one world and supported establishing a "United Nations") had 575,000 members and appeared in 2,500 classrooms during the war.

Comic books and the newspaper comic page ("funny papers" to kids at the time) shared common ground. The funnies were a major part of the daily and Sunday newspapers in the 1930s and 1940s. Estimates of the number of daily readers of the funnies ran as high as 70 million (again, out of a total population of 132 million), illustrating the importance of comic strips to the newspaper industry's financial success. Every one of the top ten most popular comic strips made it into comic books. Many of the main characters from the leading comic strips joined the military. Joe Palooka (ranked number 1) enlisted in the army as a private, while Terry Lee (number 5) served in the Army Air Corps. Dick Tracy (number 6) served in naval intelligence, and Skeezix of Gasoline Alley (number 8) served in the Army.

Those who didn't make it into the military did their part on the home front. Dagwood and Blondie (number 2), Li'l Abner (number 3) and Little Orphan Annie (number 4) performed their service to the country at home mostly by supporting War Bond drives, scrap drives, and championing democracy and American ideals. Surprisingly, Superman, the number one superhero, sat out the war. He did manage to fight an occasional saboteur or spy but not much more. His creators, Joe Schuster and Jerry Siegel, felt that entering the war would damage his plausibility, and give kids the wrong impression – that beating up on the enemy was easy work, downplaying the danger our soldiers faced. Keeping Superman out of the war was easy. Clark Kent, the mild-mannered reporter who was Superman's alter ego, turned out to be 4-F. He failed the eye examine when his X-ray vision read the eye chart in an adjoining room instead of the chart on the wall in front of him.

While the top ten comic strip characters made their way into comic books, they weren't the first choice among kids. There were several new superheroes who appeared for the first time in comic books as a result of the war who never made the funny papers – heroic figures such as Captain America and Blackhawk who flew their missions in exciting and sometimes exotic aircraft.

Despite paper shortages, comic books were available and collecting comics became one of the major activities of kids in the 6 to 12 age group. Scrap paper drives sent many a comic book underground until the drive was over. As comic book collections grew, it was only natural that swapping comic books followed. Swapping was an accepted practice that was more like a ritual. Deciding who got the better deal was less important than making sure you were satisfied with the swap. Lending comic books was a risky business for obvious reasons – it was sometimes difficult to get your copies returned, or if they were returned, they were frequently damaged. The same dogs that ate kids homework seemed to have an affinity for comic books.

The influence of comic books with their heroes and heroines cannot be overestimated. Children, on average, began "reading" comics at the age of five and continued through age twelve, when the interest peaked. The plots, while mostly absurd, still taught the values of patriotism along with actual facts. In one comic book story, Doc Strange, "the mighty Fascist-fighter," while sightseeing in Washington, D.C., witnesses the kidnapping of General McMartin, the U.S. Commander in the South Pacific. McMartin is obviously a comic book stand-in for General MacArthur, the real commander in the South Pacific. After battling the "treacherous Nips," Doc Strange and his sidekick Billy free General McMartin and turn the Japs over to the FBI. Billy, it turns out, uses a pair of special glasses containing something called "polarized lenses," a new invention developed during the war. Doc explains to Billy that the secret lenses can "turn the sun's rays in a different direction and completely eliminate glare," allowing the wearer to see better when faced with a bright sun. Developed for combat pilots, the market for polarized glasses exploded after the war into a billion-dollar industry.

In another comic book episode that came out early in the war, Nazi agents attempt to steal a special radio device from an American scientist. Once in Nazi hands, they plan to incorporate the device into high explosive "rocket shells" and "blast England off the face of the map" using "radio-controlled rockets." The story was a forerunner of the infamous V-1 flying bomb and V-2 rocket that Germany showered on England during the war. In the end, England is saved by the "Commando Cubs," a group of five adolescent boys (including a black Commando Cub, but no girl, thank goodness) that foils the Nazi plot and rescues the radio-controlled device.

To add a perverse touch of humor to the story, the Nazis speak in a form of broken German-English with words like "velcome, mit, und, der, Dummkopp," and "Donnerwetter" – the last being a vituperative curse word not uncommon to people living in the Bethlehem area where Pennsylvania Dutch is still spoken. As a child, I often heard the word used by my grandfather, usually when he hit his thumb with a hammer or banged his head on a tree limb. While the word was part of the adult language, it usually brought a slap to the back of your head if uttered in the presence of your elders.

Not all comic book heroes were males, nor were comic adventure stories aimed only at boys. Wonder Woman was introduced at the start of the war and, unlike Superman, spent the bulk of her time fighting Nazi spies. She was described as "wise as Athena, as lovely as Aphrodite, with the speed of Mercury and the strength of Hercules." What a woman! What a wonder! She was an instant hit among girls. Boys loved her too, although not nearly as much as Superman, who seems to have been her counterpart. Wonder Woman was a feminist, which seems natural since she was an Amazon from that mysterious colony of superhuman women. Interestingly, Wonder Woman was created and written by William Marston, a man. After the war, Marston turned his creative mind to other pursuits, inventing the first polygraph, or lie detector.

Speaking of women heroines, according to a poll undertaken by *Fortune* magazine in 1945, Eleanor Roosevelt was the most popular woman in America, followed by Betty Crocker, who wasn't even a real person. She was the marketing creation of General Mills – who, by the way, wasn't a general; it was a corporation. If adults had difficulty distinguishing between reality and fantasy, it's easy to understand why kids thought of their superheroes as real people.

As the popularity of comic books grew, so did adult concerns over their potential harm to children. The serious challenge to the comic book industry came nearly ten years after the war ended. Frederic Wertham, a psychiatrist, played to the media in attacking the comic book, claiming it had no redeeming social value and caused children who read them to commit violent, antisocial acts. Find a troubled kid and you will find a comic book sticking out of his pocket was a theme Wertham pitched to the media and to politicians. Fortunately, Wertham's nonsensical pop-psychiatry came after the war, allowing kids on the home front to enjoy, and act out, portrayals of their superheroes. Millions of kids grew up during the heyday of the comic book without degenerating into violent criminals (although a few did).

* * *

War created a demand for books, never experienced before. The home front wanted to learn all it could about the war and about our men and women fighting it, but so did the men and women who were fighting the war. They wanted, we were told, to fill their free hours with reading about home. One year into the war the Bethlehem Public Library responded by announcing plans for a "Victory Book Drive." The *Globe-Times* ran several articles appealing to its readers to join in. The goal was to raise six thousand books, in good condition, for our men and women in the service. Bethlehem's quota was part of a statewide campaign to collect one million useable books. As in other areas requiring collecting, schools were the focus of the campaign, and once again, the collection drive was made into a contest among Bethlehem's schools. The Superintendent of schools had a special notice handed out to every schoolboy and schoolgirl stressing the importance of collecting good reading books for our fighting men and women. School children were urged to involve their parents and family relatives, much the same way they did in later years selling beauty products. The notice read, "The book to give is the one you would like to receive." The drive was to last four weeks. At the end of the first week only 600 books had been turned in to the public library, raising concerns among the Book Drive's organizers. But with the help of the *Globe-Times*, the second week saw the drive pick up, and by the end of the drive, Bethlehem had exceeded its quota, collecting 12,000 books. Not all 12,000 were deemed "acceptable" and 5,000 books were culled out of the total. The remaining 7,000 passed muster based on condition and content. In the end, the people of Bethlehem exceeded the city's quota by 1,000 books.

Service men and women didn't have to rely totally on Victory Book Drives for reading material. Publishers produced the "Armed Services Edition" of current books as well as several of the classics in special paperback editions. The books were small, constructed so they would easily fit in a soldier's back pocket. Publishers distributed the books free to the military. Authors received a royalty of one cent per book. At the end of the campaign over 100 million copies were distributed to servicemen and women around the world, bringing a little bit of home to war-weary soldiers stationed around the world.

SOURCES

The Literary Almanac. The Best of the Printed Word.
1900 to the Present (New York: MJF Books, 1997).

Richard R. Lingeman, *Don't You Know There's a War On? The American
Home Front, 1941-1945* (New York: G. P. Putnam's Sons, 1970).

Geoffrey Perrett, *Days of Sadness, Years of Sorrow. The American People
1939-1945* (Baltimore: Penguin Books, Inc., 1973).

William W. Savage, Jr., *Comic Books and America 1945-1954*
(Norman, Oklahoma: University of Oklahoma Press, 1990).

Allan M. Winkler, *Home Front U.S.A. America During World War II*
(Arlington Heights, Illinois: Harlan Davidson, Inc., 1986).

Top: Girls' "Fighters for Freedom" series by Roy J. Snell (1943). *Middle*: The Whitman Publishing Company guidebook series (1942). *Bottom left*: Many books carried this symbol showing that the publisher complied with wartime restrictions on conserving paper. *Bottom right*: Wartime suggestion to share your books with the men and women in the military.

Popular boys' war adventure series. The most prolific auther, R. Sidney Bowen, featured Dave Dawson and his sidekick, Freddy Farmer, as the duo who fought, flew, and sailed in nearly every campaign theater of the war. The best-selling book *Thirty Seconds Over Tokyo* was based on the true experiences of a member of Doolittle's famous B-25 raid on Tokyo in 1942.

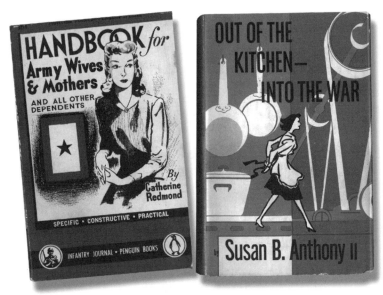

Left: A handbook for "all American women who have a soldier away at war" (1944). *Right:* The grand-niece of Susan B. Anthony argues that women are America's "margin for victory" (1943).

Two of the hundreds of popular kids' ten-cent comic books published during the war. *Left:* A Superman DC publication featuring Bud Fisher's Mutt & Jeff (1943). *Right:* A Thrilling Comics issue, featuring the "Commando Cubs" (1945).

Top: School children collect used books to redistribute to men and women in the military. (Oregon Historical Society and Stan Cohen) *Below left*: "Overseas Editions" of two best-selling novels. These pocket-sized books were designed to fit inside a soldier's pocket. Sponsored by the Council of Books in Wartime. *Below right*: A "Penguin" paperback version of William L. White's best-selling book of 1942, *They Were Expendable*.

School poster published by the U.S. Government Printing Office
and sponsored by the war savings staff of the U.S. Treasury Department
and the U.S. Office of Education (1942).

NINE

What Can We Do to Help?

Following the attack on Pearl Harbor, the Northampton Defense Council received a memorandum from the Office of Civilian Defense (OCD) in Harrisburg: "As civilians we must face the full fury of our enemies, who have no respect for an 'open city' nor an unarmed opponent." The words were in stark contrast to the attitude that existed just a few weeks earlier when most people felt air raid drills, complete with blackouts, candles, and sand buckets, were silly nonsense. December 7th refocused the public's attention, and what was once viewed as an annoyance was now seen as deadly serious. The war was no longer a foreign war. Now it was our war, and while there were differing views on what to do and how to do it, everyone agreed it was time to act.

In Washington, Secretary of the Treasury Henry Morgenthau held a press conference where he told reporters that millions of Americans were asking, "What can we do to help?" The most immediate way, Morgenthau said, was to buy War Bonds (only a few days before they had been called Defense Bonds), something every American could do. Preparing to defend the homeland from an enemy attack ran a close second. That job became the responsibility of the OCD.

On December 9, the Northampton Defense Council called an emergency meeting of all air raid wardens. Albert Boyer, the Council's chairman, announced that the first order of business was the appointment of additional wardens. Boyer told his

Council members that now that we were at war there were not enough wardens to carry out an effective air raid defense program should the enemy attack. The Council promptly issued instructions to an anxious public on what to do in the event of an air attack. Residents were advised to "remain calm, keep others from becoming panicky, stay indoors, lie flat when the bombs burst, don't use the telephone, and make sure that all the lights are out." It was enough to scare the most cynical citizen into action. The city announced it would undergo several practice blackouts to prepare for an attack by enemy planes.

The term "blackout" has taken on a different meaning from the war years. Today the term refers to a power failure, resulting in a loss of electrical energy. The goal today is to prevent blackouts, while during the war the goal was to enforce blackouts as a matter of protecting communities from air attacks. Blackouts, we were told, meant "the complete absence of light. Even a lighted match can be seen for great distances in intense darkness, and may even be seen by a bomber pilot and crew." While this warning was stretching the truth, there was one source of light in Bethlehem that no bomber pilot would have trouble seeing. It was the giant 91-foot electric star that sat atop South Mountain overlooking the city and steel mills below. In 1937, Bethlehem Steel erected the star as a gift to the city. The star was lit throughout the Christmas season as a symbol of Bethlehem, the Christmas City. Now that the country was at war, steel company officials were nervous that the bright star could be used as a beacon guiding enemy planes to the nation's number one war contractor. The star was turned off and would not be turned on again until December 1, 1945.

* * *

In the days preceding Pearl Harbor, the administration in Washington began to take steps to prepare the public for the inevitable war. In the summer of 1941 it created the Office of

Civilian Defense. The president appointed New York's colorful mayor, Fiorello LaGuardia, as its head, and his wife, Eleanor Roosevelt, as LaGuardia's assistant in charge of community service programs. It was a contentious arrangement from the start. The two had differing views on the mission of the agency. Mrs. Roosevelt saw the OCD not only preparing the nation for an attack, but providing a wide range of volunteer programs that included child care, physical fitness, and promoting all around good health. LaGuardia had his own idea of what the OCD should be doing. It should, LaGuardia said, prepare people for an air raid and not waste their energies on other distractions like community service work, programs he referred to as "sissy stuff."

Despite the difference of opinion on its mission, the OCD filled two very important roles. It provided an outlet for millions of Americans who could not serve in other capacities but wanted to contribute to the war effort. And it served in the early months of the war to dispel rumors of enemy attacks, preventing panic like the kind that occurred on both coasts right after Pearl Harbor. The OCD's primary job was to recruit and train volunteers to respond to an enemy air attack. While such attacks never occurred, it was important to the morale of the people to feel they were prepared should an attack come.

Despite the initial apathy on the part of most people during the pre-war months, a million volunteers signed up in 5,900 towns and cities to work for local defense councils. One month after Pearl Harbor the number of volunteers jumped to 6 million, and by summer there were 10 million volunteers working for 11,000 local defense councils. The volunteers came from every segment of the civilian population. The jobs included air raid wardens, doctors, nurses, drivers, firefighters, communications workers, messengers, blackout officers, and evacuation officers. The business community was asked to help in a variety of ways. Theater managers were asked to show documentary films that told audiences about the war, and to expand their viewing hours to give both day and night shift war workers a chance to relax by taking in a movie. Beauty parlor operators were advised to warn their customers against loose talk. "Information can travel especially fast through your establishment" they were warned. Beauticians were also asked to read up on rationing, price controls, conservation, and salvage so they would be able to give their customers the correct information while they were sitting around waiting for their hair to dry. One of the more prominently displayed posters warned people that "Loose lips sink ships."

Children were an important target of the OCD. "There are war jobs," they told kids, "in which you can help the older people – your parents, teachers, friends." Such a war job might be to "volunteer as your mother's special delivery boy or girl between home and the neighborhood grocery, drug store or cleaning establishment. This will save rubber and gas." There were things that we could do right away, like "save our money and use it to buy War Stamps at school; be careful not to waste anything; learn what to do in case of an air raid; keep strong by eating the right kind of food; get plenty of sleep; and exercise in the open air." This latter recommendation fit Jack Armstrong's (the All-American boy) program to a "T." On every show Jack told us to be sure to exercise every day, use lots of soap and water, get plenty of sleep, and to eat right. Naturally, Jack pointed out that the best way to eat right was to have a great big bowl of Wheaties and milk with our favorite fruit. Following Jack's simple rules would build strong bodies to help us win the war.

The OCD was not only responsible for preparing the public for air raids, it was also responsible for conservation and salvage programs. "Get along with less," we were told. "Every time you decide NOT to buy something, you help to win the war." Rubber, for example, was high on the list of things we needed to conserve. Pleasure driving was out. Car pooling was essential. We must share rides for the duration "so that no car goes on the road with even one empty seat. The empty seat is a gift to Hitler." Hoarding was akin to treason. The OCD handbook boldly stated that "hoarders are on the same level as spies."

Volunteerism cut across the population regardless of age, gender, or occupation. Steelworkers, lawyers, grocery clerks, doctors, teachers, milkmen, carpenters, housewives, grandfathers, grandmothers, uncles and aunts, and children – especially children – all volunteered to help in any way they could. Children had two major strengths that made them invaluable in the fight to save democracy – enthusiasm and boundless energy to scavenge and collect the items the government said it needed to win the war. Nothing was wasted, everything was used: tinfoil pealed from cigarette packs, fat from cooking, tin cans, toothpaste and shaving cream tubes (made of soft metal alloys), scrap metal, women's hosiery, and old rubber in whatever form, including your mother's old girdles, books, magazines, and newspapers – lots and lots of newspapers.

Publicity for various drives usually featured a well-known celebrity doing his or her part to get the rest of us involved. Rita Hayworth, one of the top pinup girls among servicemen, donated the chrome bumpers from her car. While most men were looking for something a little more exciting than Rita Hayworth's car, it helped get the message across. A descendant of Confederate General Robert E. Lee donated a set of horseshoes from Lee's horse Traveler, and Fibber McGee made the ultimate sacrifice, donating his beloved fishing hip boots to a rubber drive. "Shucks, Molly" Fibber said to his wife, "Everybody's got to do his share 'cause we're all in it together." "That's right, deary," Molly said, "I'm so proud of you."

The government loved to get its point across by using comparisons: "one old flatiron will provide enough scrap iron to make four hand grenades." The most impressive comparison to my young mind accompanied a picture of a pile of fat next to a small bottle labeled "glycerin." The picture's legend read: "From ten pounds of fat you get one pound of glycerin – when mixed with sundry ingredients, it will propel twenty-five 37-mm anti-tank shells. Enough to decide a battle if properly placed." It now seems strange that the OCD would qualify its example by saying "if properly placed." Everyone knew those anti-tank shells would hit their mark dead center. Our guys never missed.

My mother kept a coffee can sitting next to the stove that she used to collect cooking fat. When the can was nearly full she would send me to Nick's Sanitary Food Market where I would hand it over to the butcher, a funny guy named "Gike." After weighing it, the butcher would give me two cents a pound and two red ration points, not a bad deal for something that used to be thrown away.

* * *

Salvage was something most kids became involved in through their school. More than any other time in our history, schools assumed a special importance as collection centers for newspapers, magazines, books, tin cans, tinfoil, and milkweed. Schools were natural competitors and every collection drive was cast as a competition, pitting one school against another. It proved an effective way to meet and often exceed quotas.

The basement of Hamilton Elementary was laid out on the same floor plan as the first and second floors. There was a room in each corner of the building and an atrium in the center. One room in the basement contained the "heating plant," a large furnace wrapped in a thick blanket of asbestos that sat to one side of the room, leaving space for a small table and rocking chair. On the wall opposite the furnace were several clothes hooks fastened to a wood board and a large calendar with an attractive girl sunning herself. A door led to the playground behind the building. The room was the private domain of Pappy Wohlbach,

Hamilton's janitor and jack-of-all-trades. Pappy was of average height with a slender, wiry build and a full head of white hair that led me to believe he was very old. He rarely spoke and when he did he used a minimum of words as if they were rationed along with everything else. He had a low, soft voice with a thick "Dutchy" accent.

I can't remember why or how I became Pappy's friend, but on days when bad weather prevented us from going outside at lunchtime I would go down to Pappy's room and sit in his big rocking chair and eat my lunch. Most of the time Pappy would be fixing some small part of the building that needed his care. He took pride in making sure everything worked, even those things that didn't matter much.

Pappy was a "Pennsylvania Dutchman," an ethnic group more properly known as "Pennsylvania Germans." They are the descendants of eighteenth century settlers who emigrated from Germany and Switzerland and settled in the southern counties of Pennsylvania. The Lehigh Valley was home for many Pennsylvania Dutch, and Bethlehem had its share of Dutchmen. The period between 1742 and 1761 saw nearly 400,000 German and Swiss immigrants settle in Pennsylvania.

The name "Dutch" is believed to be a corruption of the word "Deutsche," the word for "German." A Pennsylvania Deutschman became a Pennsylvania "Dutchman." Many people believe that the Pennsylvania Dutch are synonymous with the Amish, a religious group that practice humility and separation from the rest of the world. They are distinguished by their mode of plain dress and quaint, horse-drawn buggies they use for transportation. The Amish live in many of the same areas where the Pennsylvania Dutch live, and while all the Amish are Pennsylvania Dutch, the Pennsylvania Dutch are not all Amish. Only 10 percent of the Pennsylvania Dutch living in the United States are Amish, the remaining 90 percent vary in their religious beliefs. The relationship between the Amish and the non-Amish Pennsylvania Dutch is their common German background and their language.

The language known as Pennsylvania Dutch is a form of German that has become "Americanized" by assimilating certain English words and their pronunciation into the language. Today most of the Pennsylvania Dutch speak "American-English" in their everyday dealings, but speak Pennsylvania Dutch at home, especially among the older generations. The Amish continue to speak it as their primary language and, in some cases, only language. Even so, the language is disappearing, at least for the Pennsylvania Dutch people.

Pennsylvania Dutch gives rise to amusing expressions when speaking English because of the difference in syntax between the two languages. Expressions like "Outen the light," or "Eat yourself full" are two well-known examples that appear on a multitude of tourist items. My favorite expression is one my grandmother would use when describing a Dutchman's contorted syntax: "Up the street the soldiers are coming down."

My grandparents spoke enough Pennsylvania Dutch that they could speak it in front of me whenever they didn't want me to know what they were talking about, and what I observed as a child was a common practice among our elders. Still, I was able to understand certain expressions that were commonly used like "Wie geht's," which means "how goes it (with you)." The stock answer, "nix besser," meaning "never better." And the expression I heard most often, "nix kumm raus," meaning "nothing doing!" or, in today's slang, "no way José!" When war came, "nix kumm raus" was soon replaced with "don't you know there's a war on." The effect was the same: "Don't ask because you aren't going to get it!"

Every year just before the Christmas holiday, Pappy Wohlbach would go to each of the six classrooms in Hamilton, carrying a large sack. When he appeared at our classroom door our teacher would instruct us to sit up straight and fold our hands on our desk. "Children," she would say, "Mr. Wohlbach has something for you." Then Pappy would slowly walk up one aisle then down the next, stopping at each desk where he would reach into his sack and take out a red apple or an orange and set it on the desk. He did this for every student without uttering a word. When he was finished our teacher would look at us and nodding her head would say, "What do you say, children?" The class would answer in unison, "Thank you, Mr. Wohlbach." Pappy would nod his head, which was his way of saying "You're velcome." Then he would move on to the next class. By today's customs it may appear a simple act, but it was not so simple at the time. Apples and oranges were not an everyday treat for kids during the war. Gifts were often simpler and fewer in those days. Pappy's small gift to "his boys and girls," as he called us, still lingers with some of us today, a reminder of a time when something as small as an apple could brighten your day, a time when everyone in the small school was part of a close family, from the teachers and students to the janitor. Each was important.

I remember Pappy for another thing – tin cans. Pappy was the keeper of the cans during the school's salvage drive. Most of the processed foods during the war were packaged in tin cans made from thinly rolled sheet steel that was covered with a thin coating of tin to prevent rust and corrosion. Glass containers were rare and aluminum cans were still in the future. Tin cans were a major source of scrap metal for the steel mills, such as Bethlehem's, that were running at full capacity. "Processing" the cans for collection was actually fun. When a can was emptied of its contents it was rinsed clean and both the top and bottom were removed and placed inside the can. The can was placed on the floor and stomped on repeatedly until smashed flat. The flattened can, with the lid and bottom inside, was tossed into a box or paper bag. When the box or bag was full it was taken to a collection center and deposited along with everyone else's cans. Pappy was in charge of overseeing the bags of tin cans that each of us brought to school each week. He kept the cans in a storage room in the basement. What Pappy did with the cans isn't clear but he probably took them in his truck to a collection center somewhere in town.

The U.S. began the war with only enough scrap metal to last the steel industry for two months. Ironically, most of our pre-war scrap metal went to our biggest customer – Japan. Between the period 1935 to 1940 the U.S. sold a little over 200 million tons of scrap metal to the Japanese, which they used to fuel their war industries. By the time the U.S. slapped an embargo on Japan it was too late; she had turned American scrap into Japanese weapons of war. I remember my parents sitting on the front porch discussing the war with neighbors and saying that the Japanese attacked us with bombs that were "made in the U.S.A." They were speaking metaphorically, of course, but for a long time I actually believed the Japanese bombs dropped on Pearl Harbor were stamped "made in the U.S.A." While that was naïve, it seems only logical that some of the scrap steel we sold Japan was returned to us at Pearl Harbor in the form of bombs and torpedoes.

The government, in its wisdom, knew that the best way to mobilize the civilian population was to make the various drives competitive, setting goals and then constantly pushing people to meet those goals and hopefully exceed them. Not to do so was letting down our boys on the battlefield. Kids loved to compete against other schools, and, for that matter, against their own classmates. Tin can salvage drives were usually set up by regional school districts. One tin can competition took place in Bethlehem in February of 1944. Schools were given a five-week period in which to collect as many cans as possible. The grand winner for the entire state turned out to be Jefferson Junior High School located at Maple and North streets in Bethlehem. The kids at Jefferson collected just over 40,000 cans, winning the state competition. For their effort, the state rewarded Jefferson with a handsome flag with the words "PENNSYLVANIA TIN CAN SCHOOL SALVAGE" emblazoned in large block letters. The kids at Jefferson were presented the coveted flag at a special ceremony described in the *Globe-Times*. The ceremony opened with the singing of "America the Beautiful," followed by the Lord's Prayer and the Pledge of Allegiance, after which Arlo Wear, a city councilman and the salvage co-ordinator for Bethlehem, presented the flag to school representatives.

The school was allowed to display the flag until another school displaced Jefferson in future collection drives. Hamilton was much too small a school to compete with larger schools like Jefferson. To collect the number of cans that the kids at Jefferson collected would require each kid at Hamilton to collect 70 cans every day for thirty days, an impossible task.

* * *

My grandparents lived in a brick duplex that my great-grandmother had built for them as a wedding present in 1907. A large, empty field that ran a full two blocks bordered the house on one side. The lot sat empty except for six wooden beehives that my great Uncle Alf kept in the field not far from the house. Uncle Alf was a tall skinny Englishman who married my Dad's Aunt Helen. He was considered different by most members of our family because, even though he was only in his fifties, he didn't have a job. He apparently hadn't worked for years and was supported by a small civil service disability pension from his days when he worked for the British government. He had contracted tuberculosis while on His Majesty's service somewhere in the exotic reaches of the Empire. Despite the family's lack of sympathy for Uncle Alf's condition, I thought he was a really neat guy because he had all sorts of interesting hobbies like raising bees and collecting butterflies and gemstones and British stamps. The family considered him something of a deadbeat, but I found him a really fascinating person. I was glad he didn't work because it gave him time to putter around with his hobbies and spend time explaining the mysteries of bees and butterflies to me. Despite my father's passion for education, Uncle Alf's diverse knowledge gained him little recognition with Dad or his side of the family.

When the war came, Uncle Alf had to relocate his beehives to the far end of the large field to make room for my grandfather's Victory Garden. My grandfather decided to convert an acre of ground in the big field into a vegetable garden to help feed the family and, at the same time, help win the war. Everything we did was to help win the war. Eating peas and brocolli, wearing pants with patches, listening to your parents, washing behind your ears, and studying harder at school all helped to win the war. Now we were being asked to grow our own food. It was bad enough that we had to eat brocolli, now we had to grow it. I began to wonder what was next.

Actually, the idea of civilians converting open lots of land into gardens didn't come from the government. It started as a grassroots movement among rural farmers who were already harvesting crops. Dubbed "an acre for a soldier," farmers began a program donating the proceeds from crops grown on an acre to buying equipment for soldiers. The idea spread into urban areas where people who didn't own an acre began "farming" small pieces of land and raising vegetables for their families. No piece of land was too small. Instead of selling the small harvest of crops to buy equipment, the owners of these new gardens were told to use the crops to feed their families, thereby freeing up large-scale production of agricultural products to feed the armed forces. The idea quickly caught on, and soon "Victory Gardens" covered the land.

My grandfather, with the help of my dad and his two sisters, planted one of the largest gardens in the neighborhood. It was so large and so diverse with different varieties of vegetables that the plot became famous, earning the name "John's Garden." The garden fed several families over the summer with fresh produce of every sort. It was my first introduction to such exotic vegetables as kohlrabi and Swiss chard. By the fall, the garden was still bursting with produce. Bushel baskets of corn, tomatoes, green beans, squash, carrots, eggplant – a cornucopia of vegetables – were harvested and carried into my grandmother's kitchen. Here an assembly was set up where the women manned pressure cookers while the children washed, picked over, and cleaned the vegetables. Once cleaned, they were passed along the line where they were sliced, diced, or pureed before they were packed into canning jars and gently lowered into large pressure cookers sitting atop the stove. When the process was completed there were dozens and dozens of "canned" jars, filled with every kind of vegetable, lining the shelves my grandfather built in his basement.

Victory Gardens reached their peak in the summer of 1943. Claude Wickard, the man who added a one-cent deposit to all milk bottles, reported to the press that 20 million Victory Gardens had yielded over 8 million tons of produce, accounting for an unbelievable 40 percent of all the vegetables grown in the country. The program was a staggering success. But, not everyone was enthralled with the idea of Victory Gardens. Garden clubs throughout the country objected to converting flower beds into Victory Gardens. Flowers, club spokesmen pointed out, brought a certain cheerfulness and beauty to the home that relieved wartime stress. Their protests had little effect, however, as nearly every backyard and vacant lot was converted into a Victory Garden.

* * *

Plane spotting was among the more unusual volunteer activities in wartime America. Volunteers were asked to climb observation posts all across the country and search America's skies for airplanes, any kind of airplane, friend or foe. The idea was to keep an eye out for enemy planes and, when spotted, alert the proper authorities. It was a simple, but effective, early warning system.

The volunteers were organized as the Ground Observation Corps, or GOC. The GOC was a civilian-staffed volunteer organization under the control of the Army Air Corps' Aircraft Warning Service (AWS). Its job was to monitor the skies twenty-four hours a day, seven days a week for aircraft and report every sighting to what was called an Army Filter Center. It was the Center's job to keep track of all airplane traffic, whether friend or foe. In reality, the only foe that could possibly be flying in the country's airspace would have to be using either civilian aircraft or hijacked planes, a problem of considerable magnitude in later years, but not during World War II. Still, a small airplane dropping a basketful of incendiary bombs could create a lot of destruction.

Observation posts were stationed along the coasts and inland, up to a distance of three hundred miles. In all, the GOC numbered 600,000 civilian volunteers, including men, women, and children of high school age. Even the blind were accepted into the service. The mere sound of a plane was sufficient to notify the Filter Center, which could then check to see if any authorized planes should be in that airspace and, if not, Army Air Corps planes would be sent aloft to "intercept" the unauthorized plane.

Aircraft identification was pitched as serious business even though there were no enemy planes that could fly across the Atlantic without refueling at least once. While no plane in the Axis arsenal could reach the United States from any home base, one enemy plane actually did reach the U.S. and made two bomb runs on American soil. The attack came from the Japanese. While the Japanese had aircraft carriers, they decided to mount their attack using a submarine as their "carrier." It was an ingenious idea. The submarine carried a pontoon-equipped Zero in a special watertight compartment. Once the submarine was within the plane's range of the U.S. coastline, the plane was assembled and launched from the deck of the submarine using a special catapult. When its mission was complete, the Zero returned to the submarine using its pontoons to land in the water. It was then hoisted back onto the catapult and readied for another mission.

The first attack took place during daylight on September 9, 1942, over the state of Oregon. Nobuo Fujita, a pilot in the Japanese Navy, dropped two incendiary bombs on Mount Emily. Luck was against the Japanese. The bombs failed to start a forest fire because the woods were still wet from recent heavy rains. Fujita made a second flight on September 29, this time at night. Using the Cape Blanco lighthouse located on the coast of southern Oregon as a beacon, Fujita flew eastward, dropping two incendiary bombs in a another heavily forested area. Once again the incendiaries failed because the woods were still wet from the earlier rains.

Two years later, in November 1944, the Japanese launched another ingenious plan using high altitude balloons to carry specially rigged bombs to the United States. Large 30-foot diameter balloons made of mulberry paper and filled with hydrogen gas carried incendiary bombs on a special carriage that hung from beneath the balloons. The balloons were released in Japan so they would be carried by the jet stream flowing east across the Pacific Ocean to the northern coast of the United States. Special timing devices released the bombs once over the U.S. The Japanese released 9,000 "balloon bombs" over a five-month period from the late fall of 1944 to early spring 1945. Of the 9,000 balloons released, only 285 reached the U.S. The balloon bombs did start fires in some areas but caused minimal damage, with one tragic exception. A minister and his wife had taken several children from their church on a picnic outing when they came upon one of the balloons in a wooded area. While examining the strange object, the bomb suddenly exploded, killing the minister's wife and five of the children. The tragic event was hushed up by the military until after the war. Because the potential destruction of the balloon bombs was so great, the Army clamped a lid on information about them, hoping to keep the Japanese from learning that their balloons were actually reaching the U.S. and dropping incendiaries into wooded areas. The censorship worked despite the deaths of the children. The Japanese never found out that their balloons were reaching the U.S. and abandoned the project, concluding it was a failure.

* * *

The military felt that one of the most important "volunteer" functions during the war was letter writing. Letters from home were the single most important link between the men fighting the war and those on the home front. By the same token, letters to the folks back home were often reassuring that everything was all right. Joanne Cacciola, a classmate at Hamilton Elementary School, had an uncle serving in the "Seabees," the Navy's Construction Battalion (CB). She recalled how "our whole family, Grammy, aunts, uncles, etc., was so concerned about him. We could hardly wait to get a letter from him saying he was well and safe. The whole family was so happy when that letter arrived, and it brought smiles and tears of joy to everyone. My grandmother had a flag proudly displayed in her window to show that her son was serving in the armed forces."

* * *

My own experience with letter writing during the war was short-lived. It occurred in the summer of 1944. Uncle Bob, who married my father's younger sister, Helen, enlisted in the Air Force in 1944 and wound up in Texas for his basic training. I remember a photograph he sent in a letter to my aunt. The photograph showed him wearing a white T-shirt with the Air Force insignia emblazoned on the front. The T-shirt made a strong impression on me. I was determined to get one for myself. Taking pencil in hand, I sat down and carefully crafted a letter: "Dear Uncle Bob, I want a T-shirt like yours. Please send one to me. Love, Bunty." I sat there reading the letter over carefully. It clearly needed a little polish so I started over again: "Dear Uncle Bob, I want a T-shirt like the one you have with the Air Force insignia. Please send me one." It sounded a lot better. I carefully folded the letter, slipped it into an envelope and gave it to my mother to mail for me.

I began checking the mail the next day and every day after that for a month. My patience was finally rewarded when I came home from school one afternoon and my mother told me there was something for me from Uncle Bob on the dining room table. "It's here," I yelled and ran into the dining room. Lying on the table was a letter from Uncle Bob. But why a letter? You can't fit a T-shirt into an envelope. I tore open the envelope and began reading the letter: "Dear Bunty, I am sorry I do not have any T-shirts like the one you asked for but your Mother can get one at Bush and Bull's for you [Bethlehem's department store]. Love, Uncle Bob." What kind of answer was that? Ask my mother to get one for me? I knew the answer to that even before I asked: "Don't you know there's a war on?" My disappointment soured me on any more letter writing – at least for the duration of the war.

Separation put an enormous strain on both sides of fighting families. Even in the midst of their buddies, soldiers grew lonely and longed to be home. Home had an emotional attraction for most servicemen that was hard for civilians to understand. The next best thing to being home was a letter from home. Letters formed an emotional bridge that could temporarily place you next to a loved one, but only if the letter was positive, filled with good news that left the reader feeling better. Soldiers writing to their wives often eased anxieties resulting from the unknown. Fathers writing to their young children emphasized the importance of being good and helping mother.

The information in a letter, and the way it was stated, was so important that books were written advising women, the major writers of letters, on the proper way to write to their son, husband or fiancé. Dorothy Sara, in *How to Write Interesting Wartime Letters*, compares writing a letter to going out on a date: "When you had an appointment with your sweetheart or your husband, you used to get dressed up ... you would always be well-groomed ... and conscious of the fact that your apparel was becoming and that it was admired by him ... your letters are the way you keep appointments with him now."

Sara emphasizes the importance of the little things when writing a letter. She goes so far as to advise women to pick the right color of paper and proper shade of ink: "write on white, ivory or light-gray paper ... you should use blue or black ink." And, Sara writes, "Never write on letter-paper that has ruled lines across the page, because unruled paper is in much better taste and style." She also stresses that one should never use a pencil: "a pen will show him that you have really 'dressed up' for your 'date' with him."

The most interesting advice Sara gives her readers is how to analyze a loved one's handwriting. It is important to be able to do this "so that you may understand fully the likes and dislikes of your man ... and appeal to his temperament." Sara devotes an entire chapter to the graphological inter-pretation of your loved one's handwriting, looking for the hidden meaning in his letters. Such graphological signs as "light pressure" (shows sensitivity) versus "heavy pressure" (shows vitality), "rounded letters" (shows cooperative spirit) versus "pointed letters" (shows a well-developed mind), "uphill writing" (an optimist) versus "downhill writing" (a pessimist), and the hidden meaning gleaned from how an "i" is dotted. A careful dot always placed directly over the "i" denotes "a good memory," while a "high dot" indicates a "keen imagination," and a "funny shaped dot" (half-moon or wavy dash) indicates a "gay sense of humor." One can't help but think of Willy and Joe, those two crazy cartoon GIs created by Bill Mauldin, sitting in a foxhole with enemy artillery exploding all around, taking great pains to make sure their penmanship shows only their best characteristics.

The real concern in letter writing was over content. G. A. Reeder, in *Letter Writing in Wartime – How and What to Write About*, devotes over half of the book to the "do's and don'ts" of writing a letter. Reeder illustrates them by printing several dozen examples from actual letters (so he claims). If your man owns a pet, "be sure to keep him in touch with Fido's new hairdo," or tell him about "Tabby's jealous boyfriends." Which brings up a sensitive subject, boyfriends. If writing to a man other than your own sweetheart, Reeder cautions: "DO NOT write that you saw the idol of his heart out enjoying herself in the company of some other man." Reeder suggests that "if he finds this out, let some-body else be the informer."

When it comes to your own sweetheart, "always reassure him of your love – EVEN IF YOU ARE GOING TO CHANGE YOUR MIND BEFORE HE GETS BACK." Reeder insists that you "do this for your country, if not for him." He devotes a great deal of space to the question of faithfulness or the lack thereof. "Resist your natural temptation to tell him about that tall, dark, and handsome man you have met recently ... it is the sort of dynamite that drives most men out of their senses." (It sure does, especially if the man you are writing to is your fiancé, or worse, your husband!) Reeder suggests, however, that a little deception goes a long way. A sweetheart should be sure to "mention a man once in a while; otherwise [your sweetheart] will know something is wrong ... But let it be some friend of the family or some 50-year-old uncle, or some other man he knows is perfectly harmless."

Love isn't the only area where a pretty young lady is urged to fib for her country's sake, if not for her man's. Religion is also important, as the following advice clearly shows: "Even if you are not religiously inclined, tell him you pray for his safety." After all, Reeder writes, "men who in civilian life had not been to church for ten years get the habit again now that they are in the armed forces." Good point! How does that old saying go, "There are no atheists in foxholes"?

In another of Reeder's sample letters entitled "Jolly for Ollie," a young girl named Amy writes to a soldier named Ollie: "The big news right now is that we girls are going to have a party in the Sunday School room some night soon and raise enough folding money to enable us girls to send you soldiers, sailors, and marines something a little more substantial than a girl's good wishes." Then it would appear the boys had something additional to fight for.

After all is said and done, Reeder is at least a pragmatist, advising his readers: "in case you can't remember anything else [in this book] – ALWAYS WRITE CHEERFUL LETTERS." If nothing else, these "how to" manuals probably gave many a girl a good laugh.

* * *

As the war progressed and the productivity of war materiel exceeded expectations, a shortage of cargo space on ships became a serious problem. Despite the shortage, the government considered mail a vital morale booster and encouraged the folks on the home front to write often. The solution to the space problem came from an interesting innovation known as "V-mail." V-mail was the government's answer to conserve space in cargo ships and keep the mail flowing to the troops. A V-mail letter consisted of a standardized single sheet of paper that folded into an envelope. Writing was restricted to one side of the paper. V-mail was delivered free of postage for members in the armed services, but civilians paid the three cents for domestic mail and six cents for airmail.

With the introduction of the V-mail letter, the government came up with another clever system to further reduce the scarce space reserved for mail even more. They set up special photographic facilities under the control of the military that copied V-mail letters onto microfilm. The microfilm was then shipped to a photographic facility overseas near the soldier's location where it was printed on photographic paper and delivered to the waiting soldier. The final printed letter was one-fourth the size of the original. This ingenious system saved both weight and space. As Reeder points out, "150,000 ordinary one-sheet letters weigh approximately 2,575 pounds and require 37 mail sacks, whereas 150,000 V-mail letters weigh only 1,500 pounds and require only 22 mail sacks." Even better, the same 150,000 letters reduced to microfilm weighed 45 pounds and required only one mail sack.

Because the final V-mail letter was reduced to one-fourth its original size, it was important to follow certain rules to make sure the letter was readable. Writers were instructed to use only jet-black ink. Capital letters should be approximately one-quarter inch high and lower case letters one-eighth inch high. Only one side was used for the message and paragraphs were eliminated to help conserve space. If a typewriter was used, capital letters and single-spacing were recommended.

Despite the advantages of reducing valuable cargo space, only 20 percent of the mail initially going overseas was V-mail. The army, in an effort to encourage more people to use V-mail, turned to the War Council on Advertising for help. Through the Council's efforts, the volume of V-mail doubled at a time when the total mail going overseas had also increased by 50 percent.

There were other features of the V-mail microfilm system that were unique. The original V-mail letters, after being microfilmed, were kept safely filed away until word of the cargo ship's safe arrival overseas, at which time the original letters were destroyed. If the ship were sunk or damaged and the microfilm destroyed, the stored letters would be retrieved and re-photographed and sent a second time. This process was repeated until the mail safely arrived.

Servicemen had their own do's and don'ts when it came to writing the folks back home. The military issued an instructional pamphlet that listed ten prohibited subjects soldiers could not include in their letters (Pamphlet No. 21-2, 29 July 1943, *Writing Home – Ten Prohibited Subjects*). One of the dont's stated was: "Don't give your location in any way except as authorized by proper authority. Be sure nothing you write discloses a more specific location than the one authorized." To make sure no information that the military deemed compromising was included in a soldier's letter, the military had examiners (censors) read every letter before it was sent home. The examiners were authorized to literally cut words and phrases from letters that they felt might aid the enemy in learning such important information as the location of ships, troops, or aircraft, or the movement of convoys or their routes.

Ned Halteman, another of my classmates at Hamilton, remembers one particular letter that his mother received from his father in the fall of 1944. Ned's father was stationed aboard the aircraft carrier USS *Ticonderoga*, operating somewhere in the Pacific. "Dad had included in his letter a copy of the menu for the Thanksgiving meal on board ship. The Navy censors cut it to shreds because the words Hawaii and pineapple must have stood out in the menu. Fresh --------------------pineapple, Baked ham with ----------------- topping, -------------------- upside down cake, and so on. The menu was decorated with a pineapple and palm trees making it clear Dad's location at the time he wrote us was Hawaii." The Navy "examiners" didn't want the folks at home (or enemy spies) to know that the USS *Ticonderoga* was lying over at Pearl Harbor for Thanksgiving.

SOURCES

The *Bethlehem Globe-Times*, 1941–1946.

John Morton Blum, *V Was For Victory. Politics and American Culture During World War II* (New York: Harcourt Brace Javanovich, 1976).

Jack Goodman, ed., *While You Were Gone. A Report on Wartime Life in the United States* (New York: Simon and Schuster, 1946).

Richard R. Lingeman, *Don't You Know There's a War On? The American Homefront 1941-1945* (New York: G. P. Putnam's Sons, 1970).

Robert C. Mikesh, *Japan's World War II Balloon Bomb Attacks on North America* (Washington, D.C.: Smithsonian Institution Press, 1973).

Richard Polenberg, ed., *America at War: The Home Front, 1941-1945* (Englewood Cliffs, N.J.: Prentice Hall, Inc., 1968).

G. A. Reeder, *Letter Writing in Wartime. How and What to Write About* (New York: Books, Inc., 1943).

Dorothy Sara, *How to Write Interesting Wartime Letters* (New York: Herald Publishing Company, 1943).

David Venditta, ed., *"Forging America. The Story of Bethlehem Steel,"* supplement, *The* (Allentown) *Morning Call*, December 2003.

Top row: Badges of patriotism. Air raid warden pinback. Navy's "E" for effort award for production. Award of Merit of the Maritime Commission. Air Warning Service (AWS) volunteer plane spotters award for hours served. *Second row*: Identification card of an air raid warden issued by the city of Portland's Civilian Defense Council. Match safe with the logo of the British War Relief Society (BWRS) logo. The BWRS was an American organization that supported Britain's war effort prior to the U.S. entering the war. *Below*: Box of "blackout" candles. British War Relief Society pin.

Top left: Victory Garden "how to" booklet. *Top right:* Government poster urging citizens to save their tin cans. *Middle left:* Civil Defense Warden's steel helmet, recycled from early WW II surplus helmets. *Bottom left:* A Victory Garden sign used to mark a gardener's plot. *Bottom right:* Women salvaging tin from toothpaste and shaving cream tubes. (ACME, New York Bureau 653284)

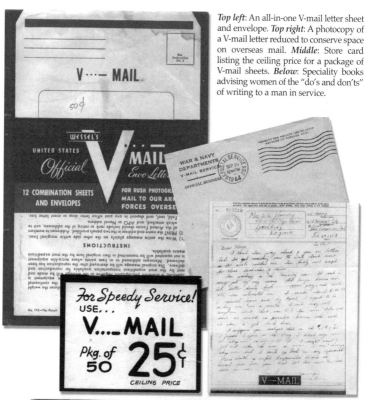

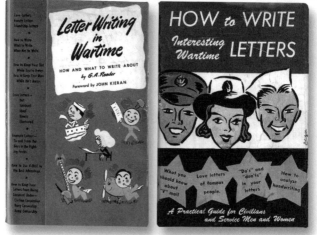

Top left: An all-in-one V-mail letter sheet and envelope. *Top right*: A photocopy of a V-mail letter reduced to conserve space on overseas mail. *Middle*: Store card listing the ceiling price for a package of V-mail sheets. *Below*: Speciality books advising women of the "do's and don'ts" of writing to a man in service.

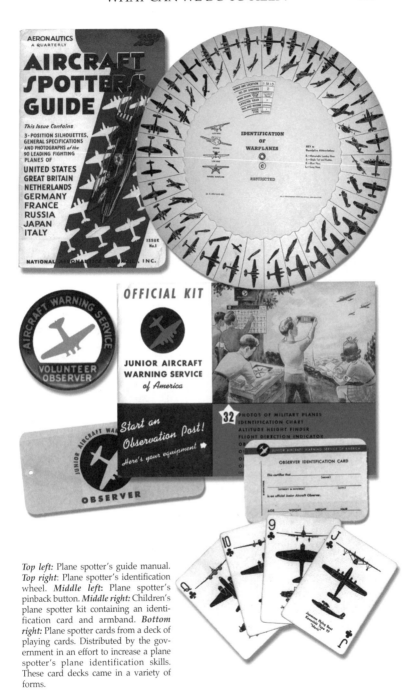

Top left: Plane spotter's guide manual. *Top right*: Plane spotter's identification wheel. *Middle left:* Plane spotter's pinback button. *Middle right:* Children's plane spotter kit containing an identification card and armband. *Bottom right:* Plane spotter cards from a deck of playing cards. Distributed by the government in an effort to increase a plane spotter's plane identification skills. These card decks came in a variety of forms.

Top: The First Lady, Eleanor Roosevelt, Assistant Director of the Office of Civilian Defense, and New York Mayor Fiorello LaGuardia, Director of the OCD (ACME, New York Bureau 9-29-41) *Middle*: Civilian Defense Guide Book (1942). *Bottom*: Senior Zone Warden checks up on young civilian defense volunteer removing rubber sole from an old shoe for his scrap pile. (Office of Civilian Defense)

Top: Window display showing what a home needs to protect against an enemy air attack (ACME 12-19-41) *Middle right*: Boy volunteers rebuilding food crates from damaged ones. (ACME 4-21-44) *Middle left*: National Defense scrap collection. A young girl deposits empty tin cans in Hirohito's mouth. *Below*: School girl volunteers collecting old keys for their scrap metal drive. (Susan and Russell Queen)

The 16th U.S. Infantry Regiment wading ashore at Omaha Beach on the morning of
June 6, 1944. This photograph has come to represent the image of the invasion.
(National Archives Records Administration)

TEN

June 6, 1944
The Defining Day of the Twentieth Century

Soldiers, Sailors and Airmen of the Allied Expeditionary Force! You are about to embark upon the Great Crusade, toward which we have striven these many months. The eyes of the world are upon you.

Dwight D. Eisenhower, Supreme Allied Commander

 The night shift at Bethlehem Steel ended at 7:00 A.M. that Tuesday morning in June of 1944. During the early morning hours rumors spread through the mills that the long awaited invasion of Nazi-occupied Europe had begun. It was a day everyone had been anxiously waiting for. Most of the day-laborers in the city awoke to the strange sound of church bells. First one, then another, and by eight o'clock every church that had a bell joined in, sending a discordant ringing throughout the city. Thousands of radios were switched on as families huddled together in their living rooms and their kitchens, listening to the news. Every station had suspended its regular broadcasting and were operating on a "news alert" basis. The newsrooms had taken over the early morning broadcasts.

At 253 East Fairview Street, John and Elizabeth Steers sat at their small kitchen table listening spellbound to the excited voice of NBC newsman Robert St. John as he tried to sum up the overnight bulletins. St. John's voice trembled with drama as he spoke:

Men and women of the United States, this is a momentous hour in world history. This is the invasion of Hitler's Europe; the zero hour of the second front. The men of General Dwight D. Eisenhower are leaving their landing barges, fighting their way up the beaches into the fortress of Nazi Europe. They are moving in from the sea to attack the enemy under a mammoth cloud of fighter planes. The world's greatest military undertaking is underway.

The "momentous hour" Robert St. John was referring to began eight-and-a-half hours earlier at 12:35 A.M. Eastern War Time (EWT). At that early morning hour the newsroom at NBC in New York was quiet as usual. The bustle of evening news and family entertainment had given way to the monotonous tones of an anonymous orchestra whose droning sounds filled the lonely hours of late-night radio. One of NBC's after-hour news monitors was sitting alone in the studio, listening to shortwave broadcasts for English transmissions coming from Berlin. It was a nightly routine and even during wartime could be a boring assignment. Pouring his third cup of coffee, the young monitor was suddenly shaken from his dull routine by a voice coming over the receiver, the words literally crackling from the short-wave loudspeaker: "Achtung! Achtung! Attention! Attention! The Allied invasion has begun!"

A few seconds later the first in a row of Teletype machines lining one side of the room began the familiar clacking sound as it impassively printed out its message. Setting down his cup of coffee, the news monitor walked over to the machine and stared at the sheet of paper as each word was slowly stamped out: "The German Transocean Agency is reporting that the Allied invasion of Europe has begun." He paused for a moment, questioning whether the invasion was really taking place or whether this was just another false alarm. He checked the special Teletype set aside for the exclusive use of the Office of War Information (OWI) for confirmation from Washington. It was silent. Nothing was coming out of Washington.

The networks had been warned by the OWI there would be many Allied feints and deceptive moves accompanied by an invasion story similar to the one now being broadcast. The Germans also were known to release false invasion stories hoping to cause members of the resistance in the conquered countries to reveal themselves prematurely so the Nazis could capture them. This was not the first time the German Transocean Agency had announced an Allied invasion. But this time the reports persisted. For the next three hours bulletins kept coming in from the German news agency claiming the invasion had begun, and still no word from the OWI on the American side.

Then, at 3:18 A.M., NBC sounded its ominous "four chimes," used to alert its listeners of important war news. Normally, only three chimes accompanied the call letters "NBC." The fourth chime was introduced during the war to alert listeners that a special war bulletin was about to follow. The fourth chime was followed by the familiar Morse code signal for the letter "V", dit-dit-dit-dah. The combination of the two was reserved for only the most important news flashes.

Crackling over the airwaves was the voice of one of NBC's correspondents in London. His husky voice had the sound of authority: "Stand by for an important broadcast. I repeat. Stand by for an important broadcast." At 3:32 A.M. the announcer again alerted his listeners: "The text of Communiqué No. 1 of the Supreme Headquarters of the Allied Expeditionary Forces will be released ten seconds from now." The voice started counting down over the air so everyone could hear: "ten, nine, eight, seven, six, five, four, three, two …" The news monitor in New York stared at the large clock on the wall of the newsroom.

Sensing he was about to experience one of those special moments in history, he wanted to note the exact time down to the second. At 3:32:09 on the morning of June 6, 1944, the words the entire free world had waited so desperately to hear came over the radio, accompanied by the hissing and popping sounds so common to transatlantic shortwave transmissions: "Under the command of General Eisenhower, Allied naval forces supported by strong air forces began landing Allied armies this morning on the northern coast of France." It was no phony report. The invasion had begun.

Several hours before the release of Communiqué No. 1, the people of England suspected what was happening. All through the night and early morning hours the constant drone of planes was heard overhead. More bombers and more fighter planes than had been heard or seen in the air for the past two years combined. Wave after wave of aircraft flew over the small villages that lined the western coast of England. Multi-engine bombers, single engine fighters, C-47s towing motorless glider planes filled with airborne troops. In the early morning darkness nine thousand bombers and fighter planes began the first of several thousand sorties over the Normandy region of France. So many planes of every sort and combination roared over the English countryside that the ground vibrated and windows rattled from the noise made by the planes' engines. The people on the ground knew it was no Allied feint. This was the real thing. The German Transocean News Agency radio broadcast, for one of the few times during the war, was broadcasting the truth.

* * *

Known to the military planners as "Operation Overlord," the Normandy invasion would instantly become known as "D-Day." The letter "D" had no specific meaning, but would come to stand for the day of decision. The early editions of most of the country's newspapers hit the streets with a one-word headline in large block letters – "INVASION!" It needed no explanation. Every man, woman, and child knew what it meant, and most trembled with fear for what might happen. Fear for the dreadful losses that many people knew would accompany the invasion.

December 7, 1941, was a day of outrage while August 15, 1945 (VJ-Day), was a day of joy. June 6, 1944, was a day of prayer. The people who gathered around their radios early that morning knew the fate of the country and the free world depended on Allied success, and they knew the cost of that success would be high. At this crucial moment in history, they felt helpless. The only thing they could do was to pray. By the millions they made their way to church, any church they could find. They went before work, during lunch, or after work. Churches throughout the area opened their doors and were soon filled with people kneeling or sitting silently in prayer. In New York, Madison Square Garden drew several thousand people who showed up for a special prayer meeting, while in London St. Paul's Cathedral and Westminster Abbey overflowed with supplicants. In Allentown and Bethlehem the three faiths, Protestant, Catholic, and Jewish, led the city in early morning prayers beginning with "Our Heavenly Father … " or "God, the Creator and Redeemer … " or "Lord of Hosts," respectively.

Bing Van Nuys, as a young elementary school student attending Moravian Preparatory School, remembers his class being led to the chapel in the Moravian complex where all the students were assembled. They were told "to pray for our boys who were landing in a place called France." When he arrived home later that afternoon, he told his mother about going to the chapel and being told to pray. She was upset that he wasn't properly dressed for church. Bing remembers telling her, "I didn't think God cared how we were dressed." Over the years it became a family joke repeated whenever the members of the family got together.

At 1410 Chelsea Avenue, Mom made sure that my brother and I were properly dressed and clean, our hair neatly combed. On the north side of Hillmond Street opposite Kunsman's field, the Church of the Nazarene opened its front doors, inviting anyone passing by to stop in and pray. We were not members of the Nazarene church, although I remember attending Bible school at the church during the summer months when school was out. The minister was an emotional-type preacher who waved his arms in great circular motions as he spoke. He had a special knack for holding his listeners spellbound. He was also an exceptionally fine artist. On those occasions when he preached to our Bible school class he would set up a large easel in front of the room and feverishly sketch away on a large pad of paper with various chalk crayons while he spoke. I was enthralled with his colorful drawings.

Mom led us up to the church where we sat down and stared at the altar for what seemed an eternity. I could not figure out why we were there or why people were coming into the church when it wasn't Sunday. The preacher was nowhere in sight nor was his easel. I noticed many of the women were quietly crying and I saw tears running down their cheeks. I felt embarrassed to see them crying and I felt strangely awkward when they saw me staring at them. It was an emotional time. People were fearful of what might happen if the Germans were to push the Allied invaders back into the sea. The terrible consequences of failure haunted many people. And so, helpless to do anything but wait for news of the invasion, the nation sought prayer and beseeched Almighty God to fight that day on the side of the righteous.

Oddly, Hitler feigned a belief in God and adopted the motto of the Prussian emperor, Gustav II, to adorn the belt buckles of the German army with "Gott Mit Uns," meaning "God is with us" (the Romans used the same motto as a battle cry,

"Nobiscum Deus," or "God be with us"). While most Americans flocked to church as a way of relieving their anxiety and seeking God's help for the Allied invaders, Hitler's accommodation with Christians was to make sure they were on Germany's side against the Allies (and the Jews who were non-Christians) even if he had to force them at the point of a bayonet.

Dominic Prospero, a barber whose shop was on West Broad Street, reflected the feelings of many people that fateful day: "Chills ran up and down my back when I knew it was for sure the truth. It is one of the best things I've heard in a long time. But I also feel very bad."

Aside from news that the invasion had begun, no one knew how it was going during those first hours of June 6. John Markovic, a butcher, told a *Globe-Times* reporter, "The men in charge know what they're doing – we hope. But working people like me – we don't really know a thing about what is going on."

Back at Moravian College, Lieutenant Robert Fatherly, the Naval officer in charge of the V-5 program, expressed his frustration. He complained to the reporter, "The thing that really burns me up is that I should be over there and I'm over here instead. I applied for active duty from the very beginning ... I'm sizzling with impatience to be in the thick of the fight."

At Bethlehem's Liberty High School, a special evening had already been scheduled to celebrate the 100th anniversary of the founding of the YMCA. Now it would be coupled with special inter-denominational prayer service on behalf of the invasion. In Easton, Judge William G. Barthold opened the day's court session with an invasion prayer. It was the same everywhere throughout the Lehigh Valley.

In Philadelphia, the Liberty Bell, reposing at Independence Hall, was struck twelve times, sending out its dulled tone signaling the beginning of the drive for freedom for the whole world. While churches opened, many businesses closed. The

Boyd theater closed its doors, announcing in the evening paper, "The invasion is on! Closed today. Re-open tomorrow." Ford Frick, president of the National Baseball League, announced that the two night games scheduled for Brooklyn and Pittsburgh would go ahead as planned with a special moment of silent prayer for the troops fighting in France. The International League cancelled all of its games scheduled for June 6th. Frank Shaughnessy, president of the league, told reporters, "I have two sons over there. I won't have much interest in baseball. I'm going to church and then home. I believe a lot of other people feel the same way."

On a different note, the Associated Press released a story over its wire service that reflected the sexism of the day: "Women Can Keep a Secret; Mrs. FDR Knew D-Day Date." Mrs. Roosevelt told reporters that "today is the day we've waited for, for a very long time," but, she continued, "the great cost of liberation made this day no happy moment." Mrs. Helen Rishak, who was born in Czechoslovakia, a country occupied by the Nazis, now lived in South Side Bethlehem. She spoke in a soft voice, telling a reporter, "All morning we cry for these poor boys who must go through this terrible thing." Mrs. Rishak and her sister excused themselves, saying they were on their way to church to pray for Mike, Pete, John, and Charlie, the four boys from their family who were part of the invasion force. The sisters were joined by millions of people all across the country.

Later in the day, the wire services picked up General Dwight D. Eisenhower's message to the invasion troops and ran it over the radio and in newspapers throughout the country:

> Soldiers, Sailors and Airmen of the Allied Expedition-
> ary Force! You are about to embark upon the Great
> Crusade, toward which we have striven these many
> months. The eyes of the world are upon you. The
> hopes and prayers of liberty-loving people

everywhere march with you. In company with our brave Allies and brothers-in-arms on other Fronts, you will bring about the destruction of the German war machine, the elimination of Nazi tyranny over the oppressed peoples of Europe, and security for ourselves in a free world. Your task will not be an easy one. Your enemy is well trained, well equipped and battle-hardened. He will fight savagely. But this is the year 1944! Much has happened since the Nazi triumphs of 1940-41. The United Nations have inflicted upon the Germans great defeats, in open battle, man-to-man. Our air offensive has seriously reduced their strength in the air and their capacity to wage war on the ground. Our Home Fronts have given us an overwhelming superiority in weapons and munitions of war, and placed at our disposal great reserves of trained fighting men. The tide has turned! The free men of the world are marching together to Victory! I have full confidence in your courage, devotion to duty and skill in battle. We will accept nothing less than full Victory! Good luck! And let us all beseech the blessing of Almighty God upon this great and noble undertaking.

* * *

D-Day was the largest military operation in history. It dwarfed every other military operation since the war began. The Allied combined forces were made up primarily of American, British, and Canadian troops, although small French, Polish, and Czechoslovakian military units in exile provided personnel in armored and air units. While many individuals played a part in putting it together, the ultimate decisions fell to one man, General Dwight David Eisenhower, who was appointed the Supreme Allied Commander.

The invasion was a multi-national operation and leadership positions became a political hot potato that required the most adept diplomatic skills if the coalition was to function successfully. Both Roosevelt and Churchill agreed that Eisenhower was the only man who possessed those necessary skills. In addition, Roosevelt knew the American people would not stand for American troops being placed under a foreign commander. Because the Supreme Allied Commander was an American, British Air Marshal A.W. Tedder was appointed Eisenhower's deputy. General Bernard L. Montgomery, the British commander who defeated Germany's Field Marshal Erwin Rommel in North Africa, was placed in command of land forces. The land forces consisted of the American First Army under Lieutenant General Omar Bradley and the British Second Army under Lieutenant General M.C. Dempsey. Naval forces fell under British Admiral Sir B.H. Ramsay, who was called out of retirement for the operation. British Air Marshal Leigh-Mallory commanded the air forces. All in all, the two countries worked well together, although there were often clashes involving Montgomery and Leigh-Mallory with other high-ranking officers. In the end, the differences that arose were adeptly smoothed over by Eisenhower.

The ultimate success of operation Overlord was due to the Allies' ability to deceive the Germans into believing the invasion would not occur at Normandy. The Allies kept the German high command and Hitler off balance by creating phony armies and false intelligence that indicated the landings would take place elsewhere. Initially, the Allies had proposed two landings, one on the channel coast of France and the second on the Mediterranean coast. The British favored two sites but eventually agreed to the American proposal of a lone channel site. The two-site plan, however, still went forward in an attempt to fool the Germans into believing the invasion would involve more than one landing site. To accomplish this deception, the Allies created a fictional army complete with real staff. The American component, dubbed the "First United States Army Group," was placed under the command of one of the war's most famous commanders, Lieutenant General George S. Patton. Patton's fictional army was slated to invade France at Calais, just where Hitler had believed the Allies would strike. Standing on the white cliffs of Dover, one can clearly see the coastline of Calais on a clear day. The plan played along with the German belief that Normandy was a feint to draw the Germans away from the real target at Calais. The British component of this phony invasion army was slated to invade Norway, thereby keeping German troops, and naval units in the form of submarines, away from the real invasion area.

One other aspect that fed into this Allied plan was that the Germans believed the invasion required a major port, which was necessary to supply an invading army. Hitler ordered the greatest concentration of German forces around the existing port areas and Calais, thereby blocking the Allies from supplying its troops during an invasion. It never occurred to the Germans that the Allies planned on bringing their own man-made port with them, thereby eliminating the need to capture an existing port. The deception worked out better than most of planners had expected. Several days after the actual landings had taken place, Hitler and his general staff still believed the Normandy landing was a feint and that the real landings would take place at Calais. By holding his armor and infantry in reserve, Hitler helped assure the success of the Normandy landing, thanks in large part to the fictitious operation known as "Bodyguard."

In all, 150,000 troops, 7,000 ships, and 8,000 bombers and fighter planes took part in the initial stages of the invasion. By the end of the first week, 325,000 troops had landed on the Normandy beaches and were beginning the push toward Hitler's Germany.

During the night of June 5-6, the first of seven thousand naval ships carried the first wave of troops to the Normandy site. The target beaches, covering a distance of approximately fifty-five miles, were given the code names Utah, Omaha, Gold, Juno, and Sword. U.S. forces under Bradley landed at Utah and Omaha, while British forces under Lieutenant General M.C. Dempsey landed at Gold and Sword, with Canadian forces landing at Juno under Lieutenant General Andrew McNaughton.

The weather over the channel was severe for the week before the scheduled invasion. Eisenhower was forced to postpone the original date of June 5. His chief meteorologist told him there would be a break in the bad weather but only for a period of thirty-six hours at the most. The cloud cover would lift sufficiently to allow the planes to see their targets. Faced with the difficult decision, Eisenhower concluded that further delay was out of the question. He decided to go ahead with the invasion beginning on the night of June 5-6.

Despite the break in the weather, the channel crossing was rough. Strong winds continued to whip up the sea into high waves. The raw recruits, crammed aboard the transport ships and landing craft, were unused to the high seas, and seasickness affected virtually all the troops. Robert Capa, a Hungarian-born war photographer, accompanied the U.S. 16th Infantry Regiment. He later reported on the strange behavior of some of the troops: "Just before 6 o'clock [A.M.] we were lowered in our LCVP [landing craft] and started for the beach. It was pretty rough and many of the boys were politely puking into paper bags and I realized that this was a civilized invasion."

It was anything but a civilized invasion on the two American target beaches. All hell broke loose and chaos reigned everywhere. Despite the lifting of the cloud cover, visibility was still limited in certain areas. On Utah, 20 percent of the American bombers failed to drop their bombs due to poor visibility. Of the 6,600 members of the 101st Airborne, only 1,100 made it to their scheduled drop zones. By nightfall of the first day, over 4,000 paratroopers still had not reported to their assigned areas. Further chaos occurred when the first wave of the 4th Infantry Division landed a mile away from its designated point on Utah. Rather than try and make it to the scheduled site, their commanding officer decided to fight inland from where they landed. Brigadier General Theodore Roosevelt, Jr., son of President Theodore Roosevelt, took charge of the men lying on the beach and personally led them inland against a withering fire from German machine guns. He was awarded the Congressional Medal of Honor for his actions that morning. Unfortunately, Roosevelt later died of a heart attack before he learned of the award.

Despite the problems on Utah, Omaha Beach suffered even worse setbacks. Because of the shore conditions, the troops had to transfer to their landing craft eleven miles offshore. In the darkness, with the rough seas, chaos ensued. Tanks rigged with special flotation gear, called "floating tanks," were launched while still three-and-a-half miles from the shore. Twenty-seven of the twenty-nine tanks sank within seconds of being launched, taking their crews with them to the bottom of the channel. Only two of the original twenty-nine made it to shore. Several of the amphibious "ducks" carrying artillery pieces capsized in the rough sea, and ten of the troop-carrying landing craft rolled over, dumping the troops into the water. Many of the men, weighted down with heavy equipment packs, drowned. A wall of German machine-gun fire met those who did make it to shore. As one report noted, "the sea ran red." The German defenses were able to pin down nearly 35,000 men on Omaha Beach. The British and Canadians fared somewhat better on their beaches.

In spite of the difficulties caused by the rough seas and strong German resistance, footholds were established on all five beaches. Wherever the troops appeared, French citizens greeted them with enthusiasm. War correspondent Bill Walton, embedded with the 82nd Airborne, wrote in one of his news reports, "As the Americans passed down the white clay road [near Sainte-Mère-Eglise] farmers poked their heads from windows. A few women ran into the road, laughing and cheering. One woman grabbed a sergeant and fervently kissed the American flag sewn on his right sleeve." In other areas the local people were not quite as joyous although they greeted the troops with civility. The bombardment and shelling destroyed most of their buildings and wounded many people. In some instances small villages were virtually turned into rubble by the heavy bombardment and shelling. The villagers had not been sure the Allied invaders would be successful. If the Allies were pushed back or forced to retreat, what would happen to the villagers if the Germans returned? One reporter wrote that when the American soldiers first arrived in certain villages the young children gave them the stiff-armed Nazi salute. They didn't know any better and the GIs had to teach them the "V for Victory" sign. It didn't take long for the children in the liberated areas to learn that the new invaders, unlike the Germans, came with chewing gum and chocolate bars. At Isigny, a small village between Utah and Omaha, the shelling continued long after the Germans fled. But overall, the French people were passionate patriots and welcomed their liberation even if it meant the destruction of much of their villages and countryside.

By the evening of June 6, the Allies had secured all five beaches. On that evening, President Roosevelt held one of his famous "Fireside Chats" with the American people. He told his listeners that the first reports coming out of Normandy were encouraging. Then he asked his listeners to join him in a special D-Day prayer. Unlike later presidents who seldom mentioned the inevitable death of many soldiers, Roosevelt did not soften his words. He spoke bluntly to the nation: "The enemy is strong," he said. "They may hurl back our forces .... The darkness will be rent by noise and flame. Men's souls will be shaken with the violence of war .... Some will never return." Honest words at a dire time when the nation was most fearful. His words are important to the story of D-Day because they came when the final outcome was still hanging in the balance. He was careful not to let the Nazis think Normandy was the primary site of the invasion. This is what he said:

> Almighty God: Our sons, pride of our nation, this day have set upon a mighty endeavor, a struggle to preserve our Republic, our religion, and our civilization, and to set free a suffering humanity.

> Lead them straight and true; give strength to their arms, stoutness to their hearts, steadfastness in their faith.

> They will need Thy blessings. Their road will be long and hard. For the enemy is strong. He may hurl back our forces. Success may not come with rushing speed, but we shall return again and again; and we know that by Thy grace, and by the righteousness of our cause, our sons will triumph.

> They will be sore tried, by night and by day, without rest – until the victory is won. The darkness will be rent by noise and flame. Men's souls will be shaken with the violences of war.

> For these men are lately drawn from the ways of peace. They fight not for the lust of conquest. They fight to end conquest. They fight to liberate. They fight to let justice arise, and tolerance and goodwill

among all Thy people. They yearn but for the end of battle, for their return to the haven of home.

Some will never return. Embrace these, Father, and receive them, Thy heroic servants, into Thy kingdom.

And for us at home – fathers, mothers, children, wives, sisters, and brothers of brave men overseas, whose thoughts and prayers are ever with them – help us, Almighty God, to rededicate ourselves in renewed faith in Thee in this hour of great sacrifice.

Many people have urged that I call the nation into a single day of special prayer. But because the road is long and the desire is great, I ask that our people devote themselves in a continuance of prayer. As we rise to each new day, and again when each day is spent, let words of prayer be on our lips, invoking Thy help to our efforts.

Give us strength, too – strength in our daily tasks, to redouble the contributions we make in the physical and the material support of our armed forces.

And let our hearts be stout, to wait out the long travail, to bear sorrows that may come, to impart our courage unto our sons wheresoever they may be.

And, O Lord, give us faith. Give us faith in Thee; faith in our sons; faith in each other; faith in our united crusade. Let not the keenness of our spirit ever be dulled. Let not the impacts of temporary events, of temporal matters of but fleeting moment – let not these deter us in our unconquerable purpose.

With Thy blessing, we shall prevail over the unholy forces of our enemy. Help us to conquer the apostles of greed and racial arrogances. Lead us to the saving of our country, and with our sister nations into a world unity that will spell a sure peace – a peace invulnerable to the schemings of unworthy men. And a peace that will let all of men live in freedom, reaping the just rewards of their honest toil.

Thy will be done, Almighty God.

Amen.

As June 6 came to a close, the Allied forces began to push inland. Behind the first wave of troops, a host of 100,000 men began spilling onto the beaches, secure from enemy fire. As late as June 7, some thirty-six hours after the initial landings in Normandy, Hitler still believed the Normandy landings were a feint. The real invasion, Hitler thought, was yet to come at Calais or Dieppe further up the coast of France. By the time the Germans realized Normandy was the real target, it was too late to stop the Allies on the beaches. By nightfall on June 10, 325,000 Allied troops were safely ashore and pushing inland. Rommel knew the truth, but Hitler and several of his other senior commanders were still convinced the Normandy landings were a feint. The Allied deceptions had worked beyond anyone's most optimistic predictions.

* * *

Three days after the landing on Normandy, a strange sight appeared in the English channel, slowly making its way toward the coast of France. It was an enormous concrete block being maneuvered by a half dozen tugboats. It was the first of several prefabricated concrete blocks called "Mulberries" that would form a temporary harbor for the unloading of supplies. The troops had carried all their supplies on their backs. To continue the fight, they would need thousands of tons of equipment and supplies. The Mulberries would provide the harbor needed to receive these supplies. The concept of providing their own prefabricated harbor was a stroke of genius, and one that the Germans, thanks to the success of Allied intelligence, had never considered. When completed, the harbors would consist of 146 of these large caissons that were constructed from 600,000 tons of concrete and 5 million feet of steel. The harbors were built to receive over 5,000 tons of supplies and 1,000 vehicles a day. The sight of the first Mulberry proved to the men on the beaches and civilians in the surrounding countryside that the Allies were here to stay.

And so, the Great Crusade that General Eisenhower spoke of had begun and men's souls were "shaken with the violence of war." The Normandy invasion was the turning point of the war in Europe. It also spelled doom for the Japanese in the Pacific. For once the Allies had successfully established a beachhead; the defeat of German forces was only a matter of time, and then Japan would feel the full force of the Allies. On the home front, people redoubled their efforts. They had seen what superiority in the implements of war accomplished that fateful day on the beaches of Normandy and were more determined than ever to keep the supply lines going so that our troops had everything they needed to win the war.

SOURCES

The *Bethlehem Globe-Times*, 6 June 1944 – 12 June 1944.

Joanne Cacciola, letter to author, 25 August 2004.

June 6, 1944 D-Day, Original Radio Broadcasts, audiocassette (St. Paul, Minnesota: Wireless, n.d.).

Martin Gilbert, *D-Day* (Hoboken, New Jersey: John Wiley & Sons, Inc., 2004).

Donald M. Goldstein, Katherine V. Dillon, and J. Michael Wenger, *D-Day Normandy. The Story and the Photographs* (Herndon, Virginia: Brassey's Inc., 1999).

John E. Steers, letter to author, 15 August 2004.

Dan Van Der Vat, *D-Day. The Greatest Invasion* (New York: Bloomsbury Madison Press, 2003).

Bing Van Nuyes, letter to author, 15 September 2004.

Charles Christian Wertenbaker, *Invasion!* (New York: D. Appleton-Century Company, 1944).

ORDER OF THE DAY   N° 4962

From The Office of Chairman
WAR FINANCE COMMITTEE

ATTENTION AMERICANS:

INVASION!

THE MAGIC WORD HAS BEEN PASSED. THE ARMY, NAVY AND AIR CORPS
KNOW THEIR JOB AND ARE DOING IT EFFECTIVELY ON MANY FRONTS.

OUR DUTY AT HOME IS THIS:

1. PURCHASE AT LEAST ONE EXTRA WAR BOND
    DURING THE FIFTH WAR LOAN IN YOUR OWN
    NAME.

2. SELL AT LEAST ONE WAR BOND TO A MEMBER
    OF YOUR FAMILY OR AN ACQUAINTANCE DURING
    THE FIFTH WAR LOAN.

3. MAIL THE ENCLOSED REPORT PROMPTLY.

Please fill in the requested
information on the attached
form and mail at once. No
postage is needed.

By Order Of:

Ellsworth R.J. Oliver

Chairman, YORK COUNTY
WAR FINANCE COMMITTEE

HEADQUARTERS
DITIONARY FORCE

Top: A promotional broadside by the War Finance Committee using the invasion to promote the sale of war bonds. *Middle right*: The special message read by General Dwight D. Eisenhower, Supreme Allied Commander, to the allied troops just before embarking for France. (National Archives Records Administration) *Lower left*: President Franklin D. Roosevelt addressing the nation during one of his "fireside chats." On the evening of D-Day, Roosevelt addressed the nation, reading his famous D-Day Prayer. (Library of Congress)

Soldiers, Sailors and Airmen of the Allied Expeditionary Force!

You are about to embark upon the Great Crusade, toward which we have striven these many months. The eyes of the world are upon you. The hopes and prayers of liberty-loving people everywhere march with you. In company with our brave Allies and brothers-in-arms on other Fronts, you will bring about the destruction of the German war machine, the elimination of Nazi tyranny over the oppressed peoples of Europe, and security for ourselves in a free world.

Your task will not be an easy one. Your enemy is well trained, well equipped and battle-hardened. He will fight savagely.

But this is the year 1944 ! Much has happened since the Nazi triumphs of 1940-41. The United Nations have inflicted upon the Germans great defeats, in open battle, man-to-man. Our air offensive has seriously reduced their strength in the air and their capacity to wage war on the ground. Our Home Fronts have given us an overwhelming superiority in weapons and munitions of war, and placed at our disposal great reserves of trained fighting men. The tide has turned ! The free men of the world are marching together to Victory !

I have full confidence in your courage, devotion to duty and skill in battle. We will accept nothing less than full Victory !

Good Luck ! And let us all beseech the blessing of Almighty God upon this great and noble undertaking.

Dwight D. Eisenhower

Top: The afternoon edition of The *Bethlehem Globe-Times*, June 6, 1944, announcing the invasion and people's reactions to receiving the news. ***Middle right***: A list of invasion bulletins from various news services published in the *Globe-Times*. ***Bottom***: A group of women offering prayers at the Holy Infancy Church in Bethlehem. (The *Bethlehem Globe-Times*)

ELEVEN

Victory!

Ned Halteman had never seen his mother so happy. "Mom came home early from work and told me the war was over and that we were going to celebrate." It was V-J Day, August 14, 1945. The day the Japanese accepted unconditional surrender. World War II was at an end. "We had dinner and then the two of us walked the ten blocks into the center of Bethlehem. The town was mobbed with people greeting one another with huge grins and laughter. We walked around until dark greeting people. It was a very exciting day, but at the time I wasn't sure why it was so special."

As they had done on D-Day fourteen months earlier, churches throughout the city rang their bells, only this time it was to the accompaniment of car horns, factory whistles and shouts of joy – deliriously happy shouts of joy. All across the country the evening papers carried a single bold headline, "PEACE!" A simple five-letter word that touched off an outpouring of exuberant, wild behavior. People rushed outside and shouted from the top of their lungs, "It's over!"

It seemed as though half the city decided to go downtown, congregating around the intersection of Main and Broad streets. The other half met at Fourth and Vine on the south side of town. A photographer from the *Globe-Times* couldn't believe his luck. No matter where he turned he had a great shot. He didn't have to wait for just the right moment. It was all around him. He started snapping off pictures in rapid succession turning one way and then another. A group of paperboys in the middle of Main Street were holding up copies of the *Globe-Times* for the camera. In the middle of Broad Street another group of boys were parading, waving small American flags and holding up a homemade cardboard sign that said "Japs Give Up." Close behind them were two dozen people crammed on the back of a flatbed truck waving flags and throwing confetti. As the truck moved down Broad Street people ran up to it and tried to climb aboard, filling every last inch of space. The truck made its way to the intersection of Main and Broad and turned left onto Main to a cheering crowd. Walking behind the truck were half a dozen boys blowing whistles and toy horns and holding a captured Japanese flag aloft that one of their fathers, no doubt, sent home as a souvenir.

Staging his own imitation of the celebration in Times Square in New York, a sailor grabbed a passing girl and bending her over backwards gave her a "victory kiss" as dozens of onlookers cheered. Ankle deep in confetti, a Congo line snaked its way past the couple still locked in their embrace. As the line made its way down Main Street, people standing by jumped to the end of the line, grabbing the waist of the person in front of them. The scenes were crazy. People were carrying on in ways they would never do under any other circumstances. But they didn't care how silly their behavior seemed. The terrible, long war was finally over.

On the South Side, the men working at Bethlehem Steel had their own way of celebrating. For three years they had kept their little secret quiet. Now it was time to let everyone in on it. They brought out the large brass steam whistle from the great French liner *Normandie*. The great ship had been cut up and sent to the open hearths of Bethlehem Steel after it had burned in its New York pier in 1942. Included had been the large brass steam whistle that was the signature of the ship. The whistle mysteriously disappeared from the scrap inventory. It had been rumored, although never confirmed, that the whistle had been salvaged by the steelworkers and hidden away in a safe place in one of the mills, waiting for the day the war would end. The men brought the whistle from its hiding place and hooked it up to a steam line and began sending a continuous series of ear-shattering blasts throughout the mills, to the accompaniment of shouts and cheers from the steelworkers.

* * *

When news came of the Japanese surrender, we were vacationing at our cabin in the Pocono Mountains on Lake Wallenpaupack, 70 miles north of Bethlehem. We had no telephone or newspaper. Our only contact with the outside world happened once a week when the milkman made his way to our woodland retreat, filling us in on the more important news. We had a small radio that could pick up the more powerful New York stations when atmospheric conditions were right. My brother and I were busy getting ready to go for an afternoon swim in the lake when Dad came running out of the cabin, banging the screen door. I knew right away that something was up. Banging the screen door always brought a sharp rebuke. Dad seemed very excited and waved to us as he ran toward our car. My brother remembers what happened next: "Dad had a 1934 Plymouth with running boards at the time. He drove the car out the dirt road the two miles to the mailboxes lining the main road, yelling and blowing the car horn, going up and down the side roads. I remember standing on the running board and hollering as we drove around shouting at no one in particular. There was great joy – excitement and cheering. When we returned from our victory ride we were glued to our grandfather's radio trying to hear all the news about the surrender." That night we were allowed to stay up later than usual as everyone sat around a small campfire outside the cabin, talking about the end of the war and what it meant.

The joy people felt was overwhelming. The end of the war

meant an end to rationing, to restricted driving, and to making do or doing without. So many everyday things that had become rare or disappeared completely would once again return to everyday life. Chocolate cake, cigarettes and whisky, nylon stockings and gasoline – plenty of gasoline, all the gasoline your car's tank could hold. Ration books and red tokens were out. T-bone steak and rubber girdles were in.

Chester Bowles, director of the OPA, announced on the day of the surrender that gasoline and canned fruits and vegetables were removed from rationing effective immediately. Meats, fats, oils, butter, sugar, shoes, rubber footwear, and tires, however, would remain on the ration list for the time being. Bowles promised that the remaining ration controls would be lifted, "just as soon as the supply agencies have figures to show that we can." Bowles told reporters that it was necessary to wait until military cutbacks and increased production brought consumer goods in balance with consumer demand. The great fear of the administration was run-away inflation as demand quickly outstripped supply. In a separate announcement, OPA District Director Frank Loftus threw a wet blanket the over the good news from Bowles when he told the people of the Lehigh Valley to hold on to their ration books. "There's little likelihood of any immediate return to an abundant supply of food and other rationed items," Loftus said. No one believed him.

In Washington, the War Labor Board lifted the ban on "pay for time not worked," informing employers they could give workers the day off with full pay to celebrate V-J Day. The steel company wasn't about to give its labor force a day off with or without pay. It couldn't. The process of making steel didn't allow for temporary shutdowns without seriously affecting overall production. If furnaces were allowed to cool down they would have to be rebuilt.

Board Chairman Eugene G. Grace didn't miss the

opportunity, however, to extol the record of his company as the country's number one military contractor. Between 1942 and 1945, Bethlehem Steel produced 74 million tons of steel. Its shipyards built 1,085 ships and repaired or serviced an incredible 38,000 more. In January 1943, Grace had confidently predicted Bethlehem Steel would build a ship a day. To skeptics it was a brash prediction. But Grace was not the sort of person to make unrealistic claims. He knew his company and his men, and he knew what they were capable of doing. The company wound up that year building an astounding 380 ships, just over one a day. Now Grace patted the company on its collective back for its incredible success. He went on to promise the returning servicemen that the steel company was ready to welcome them back. It was not good news, however, for the 2,200 women who had filled in for the men in their absence and wanted to stay on.

* * *

The war left its imprint on the generation of children who lived through it. To many home front children, especially boys, the war was a time of heroes, heroic events, and patriotism. Love of country was part of our makeup. Our radio and comic book heroes drove home the same message; we were the best because we were Americans. We emerged from the war years with a profound belief that our country and our government were the best in the world. Our political leaders worked hard, made all the right decisions and always told us the truth. It would be a few more years before the naïveté would wear off. Our industries agreed to do whatever it took to help Uncle Sam. We emerged from the war on top of the world. There was nothing our country couldn't do. Anything was possible and many of us took our motto from the Navy Seabees, "Can Do!"

But some children came out of the war troubled by what it had done to their families. William Tuttle in *Daddy's Gone to War* explained that "Nothing was more unsettling [to home front children] than father's departure for military service." "When the family's circumstances change," Tuttle wrote, "so the child's life invariably changes as well." Now Daddy was coming home after several years of absence. New adjustments had to be made, and not always successfully.

My father didn't leave our home for war. He waited until the war ended, and then he left. Returning from the Poconos in the late summer of 1945, Dad decided to return to school to earn a doctorate. His first love was science. Even as a small child he showed a strong interest in the world of biology. He knew he wanted to pursue a career in research. Graduating from Moravian College with a Bachelor's in science he went on to earn a Master's degree at Lehigh University. But it was not enough. Dad later told me he had come to the realization that he wanted to do more than teach science, he wanted to unravel its secrets. To do so, he needed the credentials of a Ph.D. to become a research scientist.

While on the faculty at Moravian he applied to the University of Pennsylvania's Department of Bacteriology in the School of Medicine and was accepted. In September 1945, he packed his bags and moved to a small apartment in Philadelphia leaving Mom, John, and me at home. He came home on weekends whenever his schedule allowed, but there were many weekends when he couldn't make it back. With a sudden drop in income, Mom took a job at Bethlehem Steel as a switchboard operator, one of the few jobs the company didn't fill with returning veterans.

My brother and I became latchkey children overnight. Mom had to leave for work before my brother and I left for school and didn't get home until after we did. Unable to afford to live at Chelsea Avenue on Mom's salary and the little Dad made as a teaching assistant, we moved across town to our grandparents. In 1947, after two long years, Dad graduated with a Ph.D. in microbiology and joined the faculty at Penn. It was our turn to pack our bags, and we headed to Philadelphia where we joined Dad in a new home. It was the first of several moves as Dad moved up the academic ladder.

My father's return to school in 1945 proved to be especially traumatic for me. Like it had done for many kids whose fathers left home for war, Dad's absence and our move to my grandparents' house brought changes to my previously stable life I was unprepared for. Chelsea Avenue had been my world. The years there were idyllic and the abrupt change proved unsettling. Looking back, I find I have no recollections of the two years Dad was away in school. No matter how I try to jog my memory into recalling those two years, I still come up blank. I can recall no more than three or four glimpses of instances involving trivial moments. Eating, sleeping, playing, walking to school, seeing my father on weekends, Christmas day, birthdays, all the things that one normally would remember are blank. No matter how hard I try to remember, two years of my life are non-existent. My brother John fills in the blank spaces for me. The year we joined my father in Philadelphia is filled with memories; small ones and big ones – even the smallest of details. In looking back I can understand how the war and the departure of a father was unsettling to many children and how it influenced their relationship with their father when he returned home after a long absence. This was the unseen effect of the war on many children.

* * *

Halfway around the world on a small coral island with the strange name of Ie Shima (ee-she-mah), planes from Uncle Mickey's bomb group took off on their last mission of the war. Unlike previous missions, the bomb bays were empty. The men of the 345th Bomb Group were on a special mission, one they had been looking forward to for a long time. General MacArthur, Supreme Commander of Allied Forces in the Pacific, summoned Japanese envoys to a surrender meeting in Manila in the

Philippines. Here they would be told the details of the official surrender and given instructions on what to do. MacArthur chose six planes from Uncle Mickey's Bomb Group as the escort for the two planes carrying the Japanese emissaries from Tokyo to Manila. It was a special honor in recognition of their war record. Everyone wanted to be on board the six planes. At takeoff they were loaded with personnel making the historic flight.

MacArthur, in tribute to the men who had suffered the terrible "Bataan Death March" in 1942 following the fall of the Philippines, instructed the Japanese to use the radio call signs "Bataan 1" and "Bataan 2." for the two aircraft carrying the envoys.

The 345th rendezvoused with the Japanese planes high over Japan and escorted them to the airfield on Ie Shima. On the approach, the incoming planes saw the runway lined with personnel as far as the eye could see. War correspondents and servicemen alike had their cameras ready, waiting for the planes to touch down. After landing at Ie Shima, the Japanese envoys were transferred to an American C-54 transport plane and flown the final leg to Manila, where MacArthur was waiting for them. It was a day the men of the 345th would never forget.

* * *

Nine hundred miles south of Ie Shima, Uncle Bill's LST 1108 was laying over in the Philippine Islands following word of the Japanese surrender. While MacArthur waited in Manila for the envoys, the 1108 was ordered to proceed to the former Jap-held island of Truk. From Truk, the 1108 was ordered to the island of Tinian in the Marianas where it picked up 200 Korean slave laborers stranded on a small island waiting to return to their homeland. Uncle Bill recalls the difficult trip to Korea. "The day after we left we ran into a terrific storm that lasted several days. The poor Koreans were unaccustomed to the rough seas and became violently ill. The tank deck became so fouled that it was several weeks before we got rid of the smell. It was pretty bad.

During the long trip to Korea several of the children, who were in bad shape when we left Tinian, died." The crew of the 1108 had no alternative but to bury the young children at sea. "Their mothers were pretty upset. They wanted to take the dead children home but that was impossible." In all the turmoil, three of the woman gave birth, making up in a small way for the deaths.

From Korea, the 1108 sailed to Kwajalean in the Marshall Islands where its crew eagerly awaited word to proceed back to the States. Uncle Bill and the 1108, however, were given one last assignment before returning home. In December 1945, four months after V-J Day, President Truman issued a directive to the military to carry out the testing of nuclear weapons to determine their effect on U.S. warships. The tests were given the name "Operation Crossroads." The beautiful atoll of Bikini in the Marshall Islands, a United States Trust Territory (now an independent republic), was selected as the site to conduct the tests. Bikini was located outside the regular air and sea lanes making it "safe" for atomic tests. Safe for everyone except the 167 Bikinians living on the atoll. The natives had to be evacuated to a new home before tests could begin. In a meeting between naval emissaries and the Bikinians, the natives were told that the nuclear tests were for "the good of all mankind" and were asked to help by giving up their homeland. After discussing the proposal, the Bikinians agreed to leave their ancestral home and relocate to Rongerik, an atoll located 150 miles southeast of Bikini. Uncle Bill and the 1108 were given the task of picking up the Bikinians and carrying them to Rongerik.

Operation Crossroads became a major news story and *Life* magazine assigned its top photojournalist, Carl Mydans, to cover the evacuation. The Navy agreed to let Mydans travel on board the 1108 so he could cover the story for *Life*. On June 29, the *Globe-Times* ran a front page story on Operation Crossroads with a picture of Uncle Bill under the heading "Helped Pave Way."

With the relocation of the Bikinians to Rongerik, the 1108 made its way back to San Francisco, stopping at Hawaii along the way. From San Francisco, the 1108 proceeded to Bremer, Washington, where it was decommissioned on August 15, 1946, and the crew mustered out of service. On January 10, 1948, the 1108's life as an American warship came to an end as she was sold to the Argentine Navy, where she was renamed the *Cabo San Vicente* (BDT-14).

In August 1946 Uncle Bill returned to Moravian College intent on completing his education that had been interrupted by the war. He graduated in 1948 and eventually wound up working for Bethlehem Steel, retiring in 1983. In 1947 he married Aunt Pauline and in 1949 their son Bill, Jr., was born. Today, Uncle Bill and Aunt Pauline live in Bethlehem not far from the Moravian College campus.

One beautiful fall afternoon I visited Uncle Bill and Aunt Pauline at their apartment. He brought out the few pieces of surviving memorabilia that chronicled his role in those history-making times. A shadow box held his cap insignia and service medals neatly arranged on a velvet background. There were a few yellowed newspaper clippings, an issue of *Life* magazine and Mydans' famous photographs documenting the relocation. A picture of the 1108 taking the natives and their few possessions on board fills two-thirds of a page. Fifty-eight years have passed but the memories are still fresh. They are not easily forgotten.

* * *

Moravian College returned to normal beginning with the new academic year in the fall of 1945. The war and its effects were quickly put behind and the school and its student body looked forward to the future. The "G.I. Bill," passed in 1944, provided funding for returning veterans to pursue a higher education at any of the approved colleges and universities in the country.

With veterans taking advantage of the G.I. Bill, Moravian's student body grew to record size. By 1948 enrollment reached 440, and the faculty increased to 30. Today Moravian has more than doubled its number of buildings, courses, faculty and degree specialties. The student body has grown from its prewar size of fewer than 300 to just over 1,500. As a part of the war effort, Moravian's role was substantial. In addition to the 505 naval flight cadets who trained at Moravian from March 1943 through July 1944, 364 Moravian men served in the armed forces – 149 enlisted while students, 40 enlisted on graduation, and 175 were alumni. Twelve were killed in action and one was listed as missing in action. Of the 364 Moravians, 212 served in the Army, 107 in the Navy, 18 in the Marine Corps, 4 in the Coast Guard, 2 in the Merchant Marine and 21 were "unclassified."

Moravian College maintained contact with more than 200 of the servicemen through one of Moravian's more popular faculty members, Sam Zeller. Zeller, a professor of religion and classical studies, took it upon himself to keep up a correspondence throughout the war with each and every one of them. He abstracted their letters and published a newsletter that was mailed every month to them. It was an enormous effort on Zeller's part but he kept to it faithfully right up to the end of the war. To the men overseas it was their link with home and happier times.

Sam Zeller was my father's best friend and our two families were close. Sam and his wife, Helen, became our Uncle Sam and Aunt Helen. Like Mom and Dad, they also had two sons. Our two families often camped together in the Pocono Mountains and sat around the campfire at night sharing stories. Uncle Sam had a deep interest in woodland Indians and he enthralled us with tales of Indian lore and would show us how to a make a stone tomahawk and carve Indian symbols into the bark of the white birch tree.

A few years after the war ended, he wrote about the war years for an alumni day celebration. He reminisced in a light-hearted way about happy times and the joys of college life. At the end of his reminiscence he paused to reflect on the young men he had known whose promising lives were cut short by war. His poignant words are worth reading to remind us that freedom is not without cost.

> I cannot [end] without pausing to remember the twelve men of Moravian who did not return from the struggle. I won't mention all of them by name; you know who they are. I'm thinking of a lad from Brooklyn, dark-haired, with Latin mischief in his eyes and his smile, whose plane did not come back from the mountains of the Burma Road. I'm thinking too of a light-hearted, personable chap from Bethlehem whose plane, punctured by enemy flak, didn't make it over the English Channel and who died so far away from home. And I cannot forget a studious boy of the class of 1933 who wasn't made to be a soldier and who didn't return from the fighting in Italy. And so I could speak for all the others. They, too, like ourselves, had hopes and plans for their lives; they too, like us wanted to live. They might have been here with us today.

Today there is no visible vestige of Moravian's role in World War II. There is no monument, no plaque acknowledging the school's contribution to the war effort, no "Role of Honor" to keep the memory of her men alive. The large white mast erected by the V-5 cadets in front of Colonial Hall that puzzled a post-war student has long since been removed, tossed away as trash. In the school archives there are only a few copies of *Aircraft Courier*, a newsletter published by the V-5 cadets, along with some of Sam Zeller's letters to his beloved "boys in uniform."

* * *

For Bethlehem, the final symbol of the war's end came on December 1, 1945, when the Christmas lights that decorated the city's downtown streets and Hill to Hill Bridge were turned on for the first time in four years. The honor of throwing the switch was given to Bethlehem's first Gold Star mother, Johanna Silvoy, whose son was reported missing in action in March 1943. Stephen Silvoy was one of 1,167 Lehigh Valley men who lost their lives in the war. High atop South Mountain the giant electric star shone brightly over the city, signaling the beginning of the Christmas season. Once again it would serve as a beacon reminding people that peace on earth would come to men of good will, but not without great sacrifice.

The war quickly passed from our consciousness, having little relevance to our lives as we grew from children into adults. The lessons learned during that period, however, remained with us, surfacing from time to time as we maneuvered through life. World War II was a unique time in history. It was a war that involved men, women, and children in a very personal way. For four years we were a nation committed to victory – from the youngest warriors to the oldest veterans. It was a war that called on everyone to serve, on the war front and on the home front. We will never see its like again.

Some years ago while driving through the countryside with my wife and three young daughters, my eye caught a tall, leafy stand of plants growing by the roadside. I pulled the car onto the shoulder of the road. I got out. Hanging from the plants were several large seedpods of milkweed. I broke off one of the larger pods and carried it back to the car where I showed it to my young girls, explaining what it was and how I had collected it for the war effort when I was a young boy their age. I was stopped in mid-sentence when one of them asked, "When can we eat? We're hungry." For a brief second the words flashed through my brain, "Don't you know there's a war on?"

SOURCES

The *Bethlehem Globe-Times* 14 – 16 August 1945

Lawrence J. Hickey, *Warpath Across the Pacific* (Boulder, CO: International Research and Publishing Corporation, 1984).

Edward Halteman, letter to the author, 3 September 2004.

William H. Hochella, interview with author, 8 September 2004.

Cinda Jenson, letter to author, 23 March 2004.

John E. Steers, letter to author, 17 October 2004.

William M. Tuttle, Jr., *"Daddy's Gone to War"* (New York: Oxford University Press, 1993).

In the Armed Forces

Sam's Monthly News Letter

Since the Alumni Association is sending out a Bulletin, we are going to include our news of service men in this issue and no mimeographed News Letter will be sent out until May.

Pvt. Michael Zuk, '41, gave us an interesting description not so long ago of his trip to the West Coast and his reactions to camp life. "Mike," who may not be known to so many of you, was inducted before he had a chance to begin his sophomore year but from his letter we would venture the guess that he will do quite well by himself and continue his development along the same promising lines as the months at school brought forth.

Sgt. "Bernie" McKnight, '41, now located at El Centro, Cal., with the U. S. M. C. tells us that he is a bombardier-navigator on a 7B-J (B-25 Army) and finds the work very interesting. He expects to wind up his training very soon.

Chaplain Ed. Helmich Reports

Lt. Edward Helmich, '32, sent us a letter the other day with some welcome information about himself. He entered the Navy chaplaincy in December, 1942, and spent some time in training at Norfolk and Williamsburg. Thereupon he was

unnecessary to stoop over so much when he walks through the inside of a Flying Fort.

Lt. John Miller, '46, whom we congratulate on his commission, says in a recent letter that he is located at the Richmond Army Air Base where he is flying P-47's which he says are "the greatest fighting planes in the world." He expects to be moved overseas before very long.

A. S. John Strohmeyer, '46, in a letter of March 19, tells us that he is still doing some newspaper work and is covering the commanding officer, executive and all department heads for a weekly news sheet at the Midshipmen's School at Asbury Park, N. J.

Impressions from Artie in Italy

Cpl. Richard Artie, '45, writes very interestingly of his reactions "Somewhere in Italy." He says, "Really it's a beautiful place. The people are friendly and polite. They know that they have been led astray and are eager to cooperate. Some of their beautiful cities have been devastated and things are generally hard for them. But they come through—and smiling too."

Cpl. Anthony Donchez, '42, tells us that where he is "Spring is not heralded with budding trees in April or the 'choipin' o' the boids' as the Brooklynite would say. I have yet to see a robin . . . there is still lots of wintertime."

In a letter received from Cpl. Ernest Ammann, '42, we read that he is back again at Camp Murphy, Fla., and that he would like to see the two Dannebergers down there too with all the other Marine officers and enlisted men. Emlie is enrolled in a special course of instruction at the Signal School.

Among the men assigned to overseas duty recently are the following:

Ens. Edward Royal, '43, with an LCI unit, c/o F. P. O., N. Y. C.

James Adams, R. M. 3c, '44, now on the U. S. S. Duane, c/o F. P. O., N. Y. C.

Lt. Stephen Sabol, '35, now on the U. S. S. Saginaw Bay, c/o F. P. O. San Francisco.

Lt. William Thompson, '37, with the 250th Inf.

Cpl. 88, c/o P. M., N. Y. C.

Other changes are as follows:

Ens. Granville Evans, '38, has gone to Princeton University.

Lt. W. C. Bernhardt, '39 is with the 423rd Inf. at Nashville, Tenn.

Cpl. Frederick Fliegel, '46, has been transferred to Treasure Island, San Francisco.

Pasquale Castiello, S 2c, is in Radio Training at Michigan City, Ind.

A/C Walter Kennedy is in the AAFPS (Pilot) at Maxwell Field, Ala.

Pvt. Lloyd Fatsinger, '43, has gone to Hammer Field, Fresno, Cal.

Pvt. Francis Spiesar, '43, has been sent to the University of Illinois.

New addresses of men not previously mentioned involve the following:

Ens. Edward Ranahan, '31, in the U. S. Coast Guard Reserve, near London, Conn.

Cpl. Floyd Jones, '39, with the 318th Inf. at Fort Dix, N. J.

Ens. Frank Tancsos, '39, at the W. T. S. at Solomons, Md.

Mid. George Stevens, '43, at Midshipmen's School at Notre Dame, Ind.

1st Lt. John Bender, '42, at the Office of the Port Veterinarian in Brooklyn, N. Y.

Pvt. Allen Zart, '43, at the A. A. F. T. C. at Miami Beach, Fla.

August Zart, F 2c, '43, at the E. M. School at

Overseas Addresses

Several requests have been received for addresses of alumni who are in service overseas. This list represents the names and addresses of our files show them on April 1, 1944. The number in parenthesis after each name indicates the class.

James E. Adams, R. M. 3c (44)
U. S. S. Duane, C. G. Cutter,
c/o Fleet P. O., N. Y. C.
Lt. Col. Conrad E. Albrecht (26)
183rd Station Hospital,
APO 942, Seattle, Wash.
Ens. Kenneth Alms (43)
U. S. S. LCI (L) 417
c/o Fleet P. O., N. Y. C.
Cpl. Richard Artie (45)
110st Signal Co., 323rd Serv. Grp.
APO 630 c/o P. M., N. Y. C.
Ens. Harold Bilheimer (42)
c/o U. S. S. Hornet,
c/o Fleet P. O., N. Y. C.
1 Cpl. JV John David Bishop (40)
c/o Signal Corps,
APO 37, c/o P. M., N. Y. C.
Mc. William Cann (44)
287th Sig. Inst. Co.
APO 871, c/o P. M., N. Y. C.
Pvt. Milton Constantine (45)
36 T. C. S. 316 Gr.,
APO 760, c/o P. M., N. Y. C.
Pvt. Glenn Craver (46)
Hq. Bty. 225th F. A. Bn.,
APO 958, c/o P. M., San Francisco
Lt. (j.g.) Robert Croman (43)
VS-55,
c/o Fleet P. O., San Francisco
Capt. DeWitt DeLawter (26)
Station Hospital,
APO 862, c/o P. M., N. Y. C.
Col. Anthony Donchez (42)
243rd U. S. Army Band,
APO 862 c/o P. M., N. Y. C.
Lt. (j.g.) Stephen Donchez (38)
Box 103, Commandant,
Navy No. 128, F. P. O., San Francisco
Mc. Elmer Davis (33)
C Btry. 68th F. A. Bn.,
APO 457A, c/o P M., N. Y. C.
Ens. Franklin Drebert (43)
MOMMAD, U. S. S. SC-1121,
c/o Fleet P. O., N. Y. C.
Lt. Harvey Dunbar (43)
70th Fighter Sqdn.
APO 913 c/o P. M., San Francisco
Capt. Maurice Foreman (27)
Unit Apes No. 1
APO 128, c/o P. M., San Francisco
Pvt. S. Stuart Franklenfield (45)
Co. G, 111th Inf.
APO 951, c/o P. M., San Francisco
Ens. Charles M. Gehring (39)
USNR, Navy 359,
c/o Fleet P. O., N. Y. C.
Ens. Eugene Greider (41)
UF 31,
c/o Postmaster, N. Y. C.
Lt. Cmdr. Henry Groman (Sr.)
Hutz., U. S. Navy,
APO 885, c/o P. M., N. Y. C.
Ens. John Grossof (42)
Aerology, Navy 162
c/o Fleet P. O., San Francisco
Major John Heidenreich (26)
305 Station Hospital,
APO 582, c/o P. M., N. Y. C.
M. Sgt. Allen Helmich (32)
Hq. Det. 796 Ry. Shop, Eng.
APO 887, c/o P. M., N. Y. C.

Top left: Professor Samuel Zeller created a newsletter based on his monthly correspondence with 212 Moravian students serving in the military. It was an enormous task that kept the servicemen in touch with the college and with each other throughout the war. (*Revista,* Moravian College) *Top right:* What started out as a mimeographed newsletter grew into a printed edition titled "Sam's Monthly News Letter." It included the up-to-date mailing addresses of all Zeller's correspondents so the men could write to one another. (Moravian College Archives) *Middle:* McArthur selected the 345th Bomb Group to escort the Japanese high command to surrender ceremonies in Manila. The Japanese were ordered to paint their aircraft white with green crosses. (Maurice J. Eppstein) *Bottom:* The GIs' favorite war correspondent, Ernie Pyle, was killed by a Jap sniper on Ie Shima, April 19, 1945. (Maurice J. Eppstein)

The Bethlehem Globe-Times

Above left: *Globe-Times* newspaper boys display copies of the late edition announcing Japan's surrender. *Above right*: A group of children parade along Broad Street between New and Main streets, displaying a captured Japanese flag.

As word of the Japanese surrender became official, Bethlehemites flocked to their churches to thank God for bringing an end to the worst war in the world's tumultuous history. *Above left*: Citizens entering St. Cyril and Methodius church. *Right*: After two long years, daddy returns home. To many young children, the absence of their father was a traumatic experience.

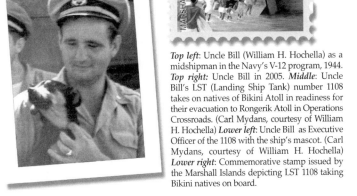

Top left: Uncle Bill (William H. Hochella) as a midshipman in the Navy's V-12 program, 1944. *Top right:* Uncle Bill in 2005. *Middle*: Uncle Bill's LST (Landing Ship Tank) number 1108 takes on natives of Bikini Atoll in readiness for their evacuation to Rongerik Atoll in Operations Crossroads. (Carl Mydans, courtesy of William H. Hochella) *Lower left*: Uncle Bill as Executive Officer of the 1108 with the ship's mascot. (Carl Mydans, courtesy of William H. Hochella) *Lower right*: Commemorative stamp issued by the Marshall Islands depicting LST 1108 taking Bikini natives on board.

The Bethlehem Globe-Times

Prepare Bikini Evacuation As Zero Hour Nears For 'Operations Crossroad'

Admiral Blandy Expected To Announce Tonight Whether Atom-Bomb Test Can Be Conducted On Schedule Tomorrow

ABOARD USS APPALACHIAN AT BIKINI (AP)—All hands concerned with "operation crossroads" made ready today to evacuate Bikini Lagoon, leaving only a skeleton fleet of 80 old warships as guinea pigs for the world's fourth atomic bomb explosion.

Vice Adm. W. H. P. Blandy, Commander of the Atomic Task Force, is expected to announce tomorrow morning (6 p.m. today about 9:30 a. m. Monday, Bikini time. That is 3:30 p. m. Monday, EST...

Blandy told foreign and scientific observers today that "we can have the test any day when we can be reasonably certain the sky is not more than half covered with clouds." He expressed confidence that conditions would be favorable either on Monday or "within the succeeding three or four days."

Everything is ready. If the decision is affirmative more than 50,000 military personnel, scientists, correspondents and observers will wait, for areas of safety, leaving only skeleton crews in the lagoon and on the islands of the atoll to make last-minute adjustments on instruments, cameras and recording equipment.

The old ships which will remain anchored in the lagoon are Admiral Blandy's flagship, the old McLachlan, and the Kenneth Whiting, an instrument ship which be working a box chock of its estimated equipment from ... a few small boats will be left to complete personnel.

At midnight there will be only 344 men left on the target ships making final adjustments to the instruments which will record the last, and light of the blast and further activity carried by the unique explosion. And on the islands there will be 42 men setting recording equipment.

But every individual ship and every known item aboard of know

Helped Pave Way

Ensign William Hochella, 23, of 446 East Goepp St., Bethlehem, has played an important role in preparing for the atomic test. He is shown as skipper of the LST No. 1108. Ensign Hochella was charged with the command of an Allied convoy to the

Congress On Appropriations Spending Spree

Fiscal Year Closes This Week-end With Many Bills To Pass

WASHINGTON (UP)—Congress goes on a spending spree today and nine members calculated that the appropriations it would authorize would cost close to one-fourth of the day's working hours.

Ready for Senate final action was the full legislative slate in order to complete congressional action on bills to supply government departments and agencies with funds for the new fiscal year.

The old fiscal year—1946—centers at midnight tomorrow night. Congress must approve bills appropriating funds for a half-dozen departments and agencies before adjournment tonight if they are to have money to operate in the new fiscal year.

Ready for Senate floor action was the full War and Federal Security Agency Bill, totaling Rs. 151,958,738.

Also scheduled for Senate action is the $67,591,567 Government Corporations Bill, providing money for such corporations as the Tennessee Valley Authority, the Export-Import Bank and the Reconstruction Finance Corporation.

"Mission Home" Delayed Ten Minutes

Captain Michael P. Hochella, U. S. Army Air Corps, was late in carrying out a mission last evening. He was due to arrive in Bethlehem, after 18 months of active service in the Pacific theater of war, at 6:00 last night. Wartime traffic slowed up his train and the depot call board shows him tardy for the first time since he got into service. But what's ten minutes—he's home and here is being greeted by his father on his arrival.

Hochella With 45 Missions To His Credit, Home On Leave After 14 Months In Pacific

Moravian Sees 394 Of Its Men In Service

Naval Training Program Great Achievement for Local College

Three hundreds and ninety-four Moravian men are in armed forces, approximately 33 per cent of all living alumni and former students of Moravian College and Theological Seminary. Ten former students have given their lives, eight in the European theater of operations and two in the Pacific.

A total of 550 Naval Aviation Cadets received Ground and Flight instruction for 13 months while stationed at the Muhlenberg-Moravian station located on the campus. In addition, 24 Army Reserve Air Corps men enlisted by Moravian College received Ground and Flight instruction as Glider or Liaison pilots at the College station.

Starting the college year in September, 1941, with a normal registration of one hundred and seventy-five students, Moravian College made immediate plans to throw her resources into the support of the war effort following the Declaration of War on December 8, 1941, as she had done which she has lived since the founding of the Institution in 1807.

By January of 1942 Moravian had determined to operate on an "Accelerated Program," a continuous college year of three quarters. Since the opening of college in September, 1941, the institution has had only brief intervals of vacation between semesters. In order to permit some college credit to larger numbers of men previous to entry into war service Moravian introduced the "split semester" plan. The terms of eight weeks each. The policy was continued until the Fall Semester, 1944, when the accelerated basis was again restored, except for the summer semester, which will continue to operate on the "split semester" basis.

In May, 1943, the Theological Seminary began to operate the accelerated program on a two semesters under the normal program. By acceleration in the college and the seminary candidates of the ministry of the Moravian church now complete their academic courses in four and two "sixth" years instead of seven years

ranking naval service alumnus both in rank and length of service. Captain Vogler is one of seven Moravian men serving as Chaplains in the Armed Forces of the United States and has seen much active service with the Marines in the Pacific Theatre of operations where he is now on active duty.

Anticipating a continuing increase in student body as the war progressed Moravian College granted indefinite leaves of absence to seven members of the Faculty in February, 1943, co-incident with the resignation of the Rev. W. N. Schwarze, Ph. D., who had long dered distinguished service as a member of the faculty since 1903 and as president and as Emeritus since 1920. President Schwarze continues to teach a limited number of hours in the college and Theological seminary, but is devoting most of his time as Archivist of the Northern Province of the Moravian Church.

Rev. Raymond S. Haupert, Ph.D., in the interim was named successor by the Board of Trustees, Dale H. Gramley, then assistant to the president of Moravian College, now president of the Bethlehem Globe-Times, and Roy D. Hunsicker, Dean of Moravian College, with the Rev. W. V. Moses, Th. D., Dean of the Theological Seminary directing the sharp decline in students registered in the college and the faculty of the institution has been compelled to offer required and elective courses in most of the institution.

Moravian College adopted the liberal policy of refunding all tuition charges and fees, except for

Top left: The *Bethlehem Globe-Times* June 29, 1946, article on Uncle Bill's role in Operation Crossroads. *Top right*: Uncle Mickey comes home following his recuperation from his crash landing on February 15, 1944. (The *Bethlehem Globe-Times*, July 25, 1944) *Bottom left*: Article on Moravian's role in the war. (The *Bethlehem Globe-Times*, May 8, 1945) *Middle right*: From an ad by Bethlehem Steel. (The *Bethlehem Globe-Times*, August 16, 1945)

radio as a source of war
    information, 155
ridicule of war villains by, 36
salvage programs, 172, 175–177, *195*
toy guns, 104–105, *112*
volunteerism, 170, 171
wardrobes, 102
war propaganda and gum cards,
    35–36
war propaganda and radio
    programming, 34–35
War Bonds and Stamps, 135–139
chromium, *113*
churches, D-Day and, 201–202
Churchill, Winston, 206
cigarettes, *113*
Cioffi, Lou, 81
Civil War, 77, 99
Clark Kent, 156
clothing, 99–100, 102
Colbert, Claudette, 100, 101
Collier's (magazine), 18
Colonial Hall (Moravian College), *84*
Comenius Hall (Moravian College),
    15, *40*, 83
comic books, 155, 156–158, *159*
comic strips, 155–156
Committee on Uranium, 33
Conrad, Frank, 29
conservation programs, 170–171
Cooper, Jackie, 81
copper pennies, 107–108, *112*
cotton, 98
coupon rationing, 89–90
"C-ration", 127
credit, grocers and, 106–107
Crisis in Bethlehem (Strohmeyer), 7
crystal sets, 29

Daddy's Gone to War (Tuttle),
    155, 223–224
Dagwood and Blondie, 156
Daisy Air Rifle, 104
Daisy Company, 104–105, *112*
Daisy "Victory Model" toy gun, 105
Dark, Alvin, 80
Dave Dawson, 152–154, *163*
Dave Dawson with the Air Corps
    (Bowen), 153–154
Davenport, Walter, 18

Davis, Johnny, 20
D-Day
    Eisenhower's address to the
        invasion troops, 204–205, *216*
    events of, 208–210
    newspaper headlines, 200–201
    public informed of, 197–200
    public response to, 201–204
    Roosevelt's prayer, 210–213, *216*
    significance of, 214
    See also Operation Overlord
Defense Savings Bonds, 139
DeHavilland, Olivia, 101
Dempsey, Lt. Gen. M.C., 206, 208
Der Fuehrer's Face (cartoon), 36–37
Dick Tracy, 156
Dietrich, Marlene, 101
differential coupon rationing, 90
Disney, Walt, 36
Mr. District Attorney, 28
Dittum-Dattum (B-25 bomber), 50, 51
Division of Textiles and Clothing, 100
divorces, 21
Doc Strange, 157
doctors, rationing and, 98
Donald Duck, 36–37
Doolittle, Jimmy, 143–144
Doolittle, Mrs. Jimmy, 145
Doolittle Raid, 143–144
Dougherty, Keith, 60
draft registration, 21
"Dragon Eye" ring, 34
driving. *See* automobiles
"ducks," 209
Dumbo (movie), *131*
"Dutch," 173

"E" bonds, 139
education, Moravians and, 10
Eighth Air Force, 142
Einstein, Albert, 33
Eisenhower, David, 143
Eisenhower, Dwight
    address to D-Day invasion troops,
        204–205, *216*
    launching of D-Day, 208
    leadership of Operation Overlord,
        205, 206
    naming of Camp David, 143
Emrey, Bill, 17

Erdlatz, Eddie,   80
Evashevski, Forest,   80

fabrics, rationing of,   98–99
fat, recycling,   172
Fatherly, Lt. Robert E.,   70, 84, 203
Federal Communications Commission
    (FCC),   30
Fibber McGee and Mollie
    (radio show),   29, 171
Fields, Dot,   67
Fifth Air Force
    Mickey Hochella joins,   49
    Kavieng operation,   53–55
    345th Bomb Group joins,   52
fighter aircraft,   42
Fighters for Freedom (book series),   162
Fighting Seabees, The (movie),   126
Fighting Sullivans, The (movie),   130
First United States Army Group   207
500th Bomb Squadron
    bombing a Japanese ship,   48
    Kavieng operation,   55–60
    planes of the 345th Bomb Group,
                                                50–51, 66
"flak",   127
floating tanks,   209
Flow-Back System,   92
Focke-Wulf 190 fighter airplane,   42
14th Bomb Group,   54
4th U.S. Infantry Division,   209
Frick, Ford,   204
Fujita, Nobuo,   181

Gable, Clark,   142
Gaffrey, James,   21
Garand rifle,   138
Gardiner, Hoyt, D.,   81
gasoline, rationing of,   89, 93–94
General Mills,   159
German Transocean Agency,   198, 199
"Geronimo,"   4, 127
"GI,"   127
G.I. Bill,   228–229
Gillespie, Harvey "Gil,"   17, 23, 76, 84
girdles,   100
Glackenbach, Irvin,   146
glycerin,   172
Goddard, Paulette,   101
Gold Beach,   208

Grable, Betty,   100
Grace, Eugene G.,   222–223
Graham, Otto,   80
Gravely, Samuel L., Jr.,   82
Great Depression,   11
Green Hornet,   28
"gremlin,"   127
grocers,   105–107
Ground Observation Corps,   180
Guadalcanal Diary (movie),   114, 123
Guadalcanal Diary (Tregaskis),   154
Guernsey cows,   121
Gum, Inc.,   35
gum cards,   35–36
Gustav II, emperor of Prussia,   202

Halteman, Edward "Ned", Jr.
                                          188, 219, 237
Halteman, Edward, Sr.,   237
Halteman, Grace,   237
Hamilton Elementary School,
                    133–135, 172–173, 174–176
Hanson, Arthur G.,   80
Hargrove, Marion,   154
Hayward, Susan,   101
Hayworth, Rita,   101, 171
helicopters,   33
Hestor, James,   80
Heydt, Harold and Joyce,   117
high altitude balloons,   181–182
Hill to Hill Bridge,   21–22, 61, 231
Hirsch, Elroy,   80
Hitler, Adolf
    banning of MGM films,   125
    Normandy invasion and,   207, 213
    religion and,   202–203
    ridiculing of,   36–37
hoarding,   171
Hochella, Andy,   8, 51
Hochella, Bill, Jr.,   228
Hochella, Elwood,   51, 52
Hochella, Ethyl,   51
Hochella, Mary,   8, 51, 52
Hochella, Michael F. "Mickey" in the
Army Air Corps,
                        23, 49, 50, 51–53, 66, 67
    Bethlehem Globe-Times article on, 236
    childhood,   51
    crash and rescue,   55–60
    Kavieng operation,   53–60

return to Bethlehem, 60–64
Hochella, Pauline, 228
Hochella, William H. "Bill,"
        52, 82, 226–228, *235, 236*
Hollywood. *See* movie industry
Hollywood at War
    (Jones and McClure), 116
Holy Infancy Church, *217*
home deliveries, 38–39
Hope, Bob, 155
Hop Harrigan, 28, 41–42, *47*, 50, 116
Hornet (aircraft carrier), 143–144
Howard, John, 58
Howard University, 81
How to Dress in Wartime
    (Rauschenbush), 100
*How to Write Interesting Wartime
    Letters* (Sara), 184–185
Hughs, Harry R., 80

I Never Left Home (Hope), 155
Ie Shima, 225–226
inflatable vests, 127
International League, 204
internment camps, 21
Isigny (France), 210

Jack Armstrong, *24*, 28, 32–34, 170
Japan
    airplane bombing of the U.S.,
                            180–181
        balloon bombs, 181–182
        U.S. scrap metal and, 176
Japanese-Americans, 21
jargon, 126–127
"Java," 127
Jefferson Junior High School, 177
Jensen, Cinda, *237*
Jimmy Allen, *24*, 50
Joe Palooka, 156
Johnson, Lt. Carl, 70
Jones, Ken, 116
Jordan, Jim and Marion, 29
kapok, 103–104
Kato, 28
Kavieng operation, 53–60, *68, 69*
KDKA radio station, 29
Kennedy, Robert F., 80
Kenney, Major Gen. George C., 52
King, Edward J., 80

knickers, 102
Knox, Frank, 75
Korean slave laborers, 226–227
Kuhn, Bowie, 80
Kunsman's field, 26–27, *45*
Kurtz (movie theater), 116

LaGuardia, Fiorello, 169, *194*
Laird, Melvin, 80
Leahy, Frank, 80
"leg make-up," 101
Lehigh University, 9, 10
Lehigh Valley, 173
Lehigh Valley Transportation
    Company (LVT), 98
Leigh-Mallory, Trafford, 206
letter writing, 182–188, *192*
Letter Writing in Wartime (Reeder),
                            185–186
Liberty Bell, 203
libraries, 152, 154, 159
library reading programs, 152
license plates, *113*
life floats (rafts), 137
Life (magazine), 227
life preservers, 103
Li'l Abner 156
Lingayen Gulf, 22
Little Orphan Annie, *47*, 156
Loftus, Frank, 222
Lombard, Carol, 101, 142
The Lone Ranger, 28, 31–32, 35, *47*
Loo, Richard, 116, *130*
Louis, Joe "Brown Bomber," 19–20
LST 1108 (Landing Ship Tank),
                82, 226–228, *235*
Lucky Strike cigarettes, *113*
Luke, Keye, 126
Luzon (Philippines), 22

MacArthur, Gen. Douglas,
            22, 49, 52, 53, 225–226
machine guns, 54, 63
"Mae West," 127
mail, 186–188, *192*
Majczan, Stan, 17
Markovic, John, 203
Marshall Islands, 227
Marston, William, 158
Mathias, Charles "Mac," Jr., 80

Mayer, Alan, 19
McCain, John III, 145
McCain, John S., 145
McCain, John S., Jr., 145
McClure, Arthur, 116
McCormick, Robert, 80
McEndy, Lt. Commander, *70*
McNaughton, Lt. Gen. Andrew, 208
medical care, rationing and, 98
Merchant Marine, 126
MGM films, 125
microfilm, 187
milk bottles, 119–122, *129*
milkweed, 103
missionaries, Moravian, 9–10
Mitchell, Thomas, 123
Montgomery, Gen. Bernard L., 206
Moravian Book Shop, 151–152
Moravian College
    Colonial Hall, *84*
    Comenius Hall, *15*, 40, 83
    decline in student numbers, 71–72
    faculty wives, *15*
    history of, 10
    Navy "V" program and,
        71, 75–78, 82–83, *84*, *85*
    postwar growth and change,
        228–229, 230–231
    Steers family and, 10–11, *15*
Moravian College and Theological
    Seminary, 10
Moravian College *Greyhounds*, 17
Moravian Ministerial Pension Fund,
        151
Moravians, 9–10
Morgan, Frank, 124
Morgenthau, Henry, Jr., *132*, 139, 167
Morse code, 76–77
Mortal Storm, The (movie), 124, *131*
movie industry
    aircraft carrier *Shangri-La* and,
        129, 143–145
    War Bonds and, 142–143
    wartime movie production,
        116, 122, 124
movies
    anti-Fascist, 124–125
    Office of War Information and, 124
    popularity of, 115
    promoting War Bonds, 143

serials, 125–126
    wartime numbers of, 124
    See also war movies
movie theaters
    Boyd theater, 116–119, *129*, 204
    number of, 124
    volunteerism and, 169–170
    War Bonds and, 142–143
Moynihan, Daniel P., 80
Muhlenberg College, 75
"Mulberries," 213–214
Murphy, George, 123
Mydans, Carl, 227

National Baseball League, 204
National Broadcasting Company
    announcing of D-Day, 197–200
    splitting of, 30
National Tire Registration Week, 95
Nazareth High School, 138
Nazareth (PA), 138
Nelson, Barry, 123
New Britain, 53, *68*
New Guinea, 52, 53
New Ireland, 53, *68*
newspaper boys, *234*
newspapers, comic strips, 155–156
New York Times, 123
Nick's Sanitary Food Market,
        105, *109*, 121–122, 172
Nolan, Lloyd, 123
nonfiction books, 154–155, 159
Normandie (ocean liner), 220–221
Normandie (ship), 103–104
Normandy invasion.
    See D-Day; Operation Overlord
North American B-25 bombers
    Doolittle Raid, 143–144
    Mickey Hochella and,
        49, 50, 51, 52, 62–63
    naming of planes, 50
    Stubborn Hellion, 51, 54–57, *67*
    38th Bomb Group, 54
    See also 345th Bomb Group
Northampton County Prison, 145–146
Northampton Defense Council,
        167–168
nuclear weapons. *See* atom bombs
nylon stockings, 101–102

Oestreicher, Elda, 134–135
Office of Civilian Defense (OCD), 167, 168–172, *194*
Office of Defense Transportation (ODT), 95, 97
Office of Price Administration (OPA), 88, 89, 92, 96, 105–106, 222
Office of War Information (OWI), *86*, 124, 199
Okinawa, 145
oleomargarine ("oleo"), 103
Omaha Beach, *196*, 208, 209
101st Airborne, 209
One World (Wilkie), 154–155
Operation "Bodyguard," 207
Operation Cartwheel, 52
Operation Crossroads, 227–228, *236*
Operation Overlord
    countries providing troops for, 205
    leadership in, 205–206
    man-made harbors, 213–214
    number of troops involved in, 207
    planning and deceiving
        the Germans, 206–207
    See also D-Day
Orr, William, 124

"parafrags" (parachute fragmentation bombs), 54
payroll deduction plan, for
    purchasing War Bonds, 140–142
Pearl Harbor
    Japanese attack, 17–18
    Roosevelt's statements following, 20–21
pennies, 107–108, *112*
Pennsylvania Dutch, 173–174
Pennsylvania Germans, 173
Pennsylvania Interscholastic
    Athletic Association, 97
penny script, *112*
Philippine Islands, 22, 33–34, 53, 225–226
Phillian, Gregory, 11
"Pilot's Mascot" (button), 49
Pittsburgh (PA), 29
plane spotting, 77–78, 180, *193*
point rationing, 89
polling, in radio, 41
Port Moresby (New Guinea), 52

posters
    Office of War Information and, *86*
    War Savings Bonds and, 140, *149*
    War Saving Stamp program and, 137, *148*
    wartime movies, *114, 129, 130, 131*
Power, Tyrone, 143
premium giveaways, 37–38, 41–44
price controls, 87–88
Produce & Conserve, Share & Play Fair (Ward), 108
propaganda
    anti-Fascist movies, 124–125
    See also war propaganda
Prospero, Dominic, 203
publishers. *See* book industry
Purple Heart, The (movie), *129, 130*
Pyle, Ernie, *233*

Quaker Oats Company, 42–43

Rabaul, *68*
race, Navy "V" program and, 81–82
radio
    beginnings and growth
        of broadcasting, 29
    children's programming
        and war propaganda, 34–35
    children's source of
        war information, 155
    hero programs and characters, *24*, 28, 31–34
    independents, 30–31
    major networks, 30
    markets and programming, 30
    premium giveaways, 37–38, 41–44
    "premium polls," 41
    public interest in aviation and, 49–50
radio broadcasting networks, 30
radio stations, 29
Ramsay, Adm. B.H., 206
ration bank accounts, 90
ration boards, 88
ration books, 90–91, 98, *110*
ration coupons, *110*
ration "currency," 90
rationing
    black marketeers and, 19, 91–92
    of car tires, 94–95

citizen response to, 88
commodities affected, 89
controls, 88–89, 92
effect of, 19
end of, 107–108
exceptions, 93
of fabrics, 98–99
of gasoline, 89, 93–94
grocers and, 105–107
making change, 92–93
of medical care, 98
reason for, 87
substituted products, 103–105, 112
success of, 108
types of, 89–90
V-J Day and, 222
ration points, 89
Rauschenbush, Winifred, 100
Red Network, 30
"Red Ryder" B-B gun, 105
Reeder, G.A., 185–186
religion
Hitler and, 202–203
See also churches
rings, radio heroes and, 34
Rishak, Helen, 204
Robinson, Edward G., 124
Robinson, Lt. R., 70
Rogers, Ginger, 101
Romans, 202–203
Rommel, Erwin, 213
Roosevelt, Eleanor, 158, 169, 194, 204
Roosevelt, Franklin Delano
blacks in the U.S. Navy and, 81
D-Day prayer, 210–213, 216
Doolittle Raid and, 144
end of Great Depression and, 11
Navy "V" program and, 74, 81
Operation Overlord and, 206
rationing and, 88
Shangri-La retreat of, 143
statement following Pearl Harbor, 20–21
Roosevelt, Brig. Gen. Theodore, Jr., 209
Rose, Robert, 123
Rosen, Al, 80
Rowan, Carl T., 81, 82
rubber, 94–95, 170–171
Rudolph, William "Uncle Willy," 237

St. John, Robert, 197–198
Salamaua (New Guinea), 53
Salinger, Pierre, 80
salvage programs,
170, 171–172, 175–177, 191
Sam's Monthly News Letter, 233
Sanitary Food Market,
105, 109, 121–122, 172
Sara, Dorothy, 184–185
schools
Hamilton Elementary,
133–135, 172–173, 174–176
Jefferson Junior High, 177
Nazareth High, 138
salvage drives, 172, 175–177, 195
Victory Book Drives, 159–160
War Stamps and Bonds, 135–139
Schuster, Joe, 156
Scott, Martha, 101
scrap metal
collecting old keys, 195
supplies, following Pearl Harbor,
176
tin can salvage drives, 175–177, 191
Seabees, 126
Sears, Roebuck, 94–95
Seaton, George, 31
2nd Carrier Task Force, 145
Secret Agent X-9 (movie serial),
126, 130
See Here Private Hargrove (Hargrove),
154
Seifert, Ella, 105
Seifert's Store, 105, 106–107, 109
semaphore, 77
serials, 125–126
The Shadow, 34, 45
Shangri-La (aircraft carrier),
129, 143–145
Shangri-La (FDR's presidential
retreat), 143
Sheridan, Ann, 101
shipyards, 7
Shirer, William L., 154
shoes, 102
Shaughnessy, Frank, 204
Siegel, Jerry, 156
silk, 98
Silvoy, Johanna, 231
16th U.S. Infantry Regiment, 196, 208

Skeezix (Gasoline Alley), 156
slack costumes, 100
slang, 126–127
Slovaks, 8
Smith, Kate, 142
"The Smith Family" (radio show), 29
"snafu," 127
soap operas, 29, 30
songs
    naming of bombers and, 50
    promoting War Bonds, 132, 145
South Bethlehem (PA), 8
soybeans, 113
speed limits, 96
spotter wheels, 77
Stack, Robert, 124
"Star of Bethlehem," 12, 13, 168, 231
Sainte-Mère-Eglise (France), 210
steel industry, 7
    See also Bethlehem Steel
Steers, Edward, Sr., 15
    academic career, 224–225
    domestic life, 2–3, 6
    at Moravian College, 10–11
    Navy "V" program and,
        76, 77, 78, 84
Steers, Elizabeth, 197
Steers, John (grandfather), 8, 197
Steers, John, 1, 2, 5–6, 11, 14, 224
Steers, Mary Beth, 11
Stewart, Jimmy, 124, 125
Stocker, Ernest, 97
"Stocking Stick," 101, 113
Stone, Marvin, 81
Striker, Fran, 31
Stroheim, Erich von, 116
Strohmeyer, John, 7, 81
Stubborn Hellion (B-25 bomber),
        51, 54–57, 67
Styron, William, 81
submarines, 180–181
sugar, rationing of, 89, 91
suits, 99
Sullavan, Margaret, 125
Superman, 37, 46, 156
Sword Beach, 208
synthetic fabrics, 98–99

tanks, 209
Tank Tinker, 28

Tatum, Jim, 80
Taylor, Robert, 115, 123
Tedder, A. W., 206
Terry Lee, 28, 42, 64, 156
theological seminary, 10
They Were Expendable (White), 154
38th Bomb Group, 54
Thirty Seconds Over Tokyo (Lawson), 163
351st Bomb Group, 142
345th Bomb Group
    "C" flight, 50–51
    Kavieng operation, 54–60
    mission escorting Japanese envoys,
        225–226, 233
    Salamaua operation, 52–53
"Three Little Fishes" (song), 50
Ticonderoga (aircraft carrier), 188
tin cans and tin salvaging, 175–177, 191
tire certificates, 111
tires
    rationing and, 89, 111
    wartime conservation of
        rubber and, 94–95
Tokyo raid. See Doolittle Raid
Tom Mix, 28, 32, 47
toy guns, 104–105, 112
Transocean Agency, 198, 199
travel restrictions, 96–97
Tregaskis, Richard, 123, 154
Trendle, George W., 31–32
trolleys, 98
Truman, Harry, 227
Tuttle, William M., Jr., 155, 223–224

Under Cover (Carlson), 154
uniform coupon rationing, 89–90
Unitas Fratrum, 9
U.S. Mint, 107–108
U.S. Navy
    post-Pearl Harbor buildup, 72–73
    Seabees, 126
    "V" program,
        71, 73–78, 80–82, 84, 85
Unity of Brethren, 9
uranium, 33
Utah Beach, 208–209

vacant lots, 26–27
Van Nuys, Bing, 26, 135, 201
vaudeville, on radio, 29

Victory Book Drives,   159–160
"Victory Cent,"   112
Victory Gardens,   178–179, 191
"Victory Suit,"   99
V-J Day,   219–222, 234
V-mail,   186–188, 192
volunteers and volunteerism
    businesses and,   169–170
    children and,   170, 171
    conservation programs,   170–171
    numbers of,   169
    Office of Civilian Defense, 168–169
    plane spotting,   179–180
    salvage programs,
        170, 171–172, 175–177, 191, 195
Victory Gardens,   178–179, 191
von Stroheim, Erich,   116
V program,   71, 73–78, 80–82, 85
V-1 program,   73
V-5 program,   74–78, 85
V-7 program,   73
V-12 program,   73, 74, 75, 80, 82

Wainwright, Gen. Jonathan,   22
Wake Island (movie),   115, 131
Walker, Robert,   123
"walkie-talkie,"   127
Walton, Bill,   210
War Advertising Council, 139–140, 187
Ward, Barbara McLean,   108
War Finance Committee,   139, 216
War Food Administration (WFA),   88
war jargon,   126–127
War Labor Board,   222
war movies
    characteristics of,   115, 122
    educational value,   126
    "hiss and boo" variety,   116
    impressions left by,   123–124
    numbers of,   124
    posters and advertisements,
                114, 129, 130, 131
    stereotyping in,   122–123
    war jargon and,   126–127
War Production Board (WPB),   88, 99
war propaganda
    gum cards for children and, 35–36
    radio programming for
        children and,   34–35
    See also propaganda

War Ration Book One,   90–91, 110
War Ration Book Two,   91
War Ration Book Three,   98, 110, 111
War Ration Book Four,   111
War Savings Bonds,   147, 148, 149
    bond drives,   139, 142
    movie industry and,   142–143
    Northampton County Prison and,
                                145–146
    payroll deduction plan,   140–142
    promoting, 132, 139–140, 145, 167
    purpose of,   139
    school War Stamp program and,
                                136–139
War Savings Stamps,
            135–138, 147, 148, 149
war violence
    gum cards and,   35–36, 47
    radio shows for children and, 35
Welles, Orson,   140
WENR radio station,   29
Wertham, Frederic,   159
West, Mae,   127
Westinghouse Corporation,   29
Whattum-Choo (B-25 bomber),   50
White, William L.,   154
Whitman Publishing Company,   162
Wholbach, "Pappy,"
            172–173, 174–175, 176
Wicht, Ed,   97
Wickard, Claude R.,   119, 179
Wicker, Tom,   81
"wigwag",   77
Wilkie, Wendell,   154–155
Williams, Roger,   81
"William Tell Overture,"   31
Willimet, Henry,   21
Wimmer, Herbert "Mr. Sunshine,"
                             39–41, 45
women
    heroines,   158–159
    jobs at Bethlehem Steel,   223
    letter writing and,   184–186
    wardrobe-related shortages, 99–102
Wonder Woman,   158
Wood, Richard D.,   81
wool,   98, 99
WXYZ radio station,   31
Wyeth, N.C.,   151

Young, Loretta, 101
Young, Robert, 124, 125

Zeller, Samuel, 229–230, 233
zinc pennies, 107, 112

Zinzendorf, Count Nikolaus
    Ludwig von, 9, 10
"Zoot Suit," 127, 128
Zumas, Nick, 19, 105, 121–122
Zumberge, James H., 80

OTHER BOOKS BY

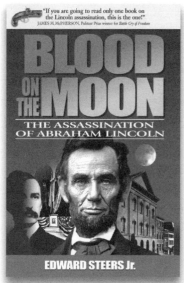

University Press of Kentucky
ISBN-13: 978-0813191515

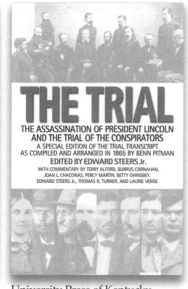

University Press of Kentucky
ISBN-13: 978-0813122779

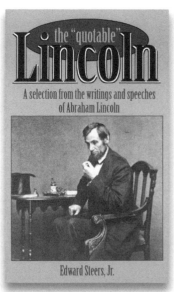

Thomas Publications
ISBN-13: 978-157747000

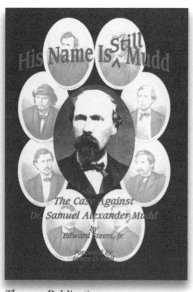

Thomas Publications
ISBN-13: 978-157747025

EDWARD STEERS, Jr.

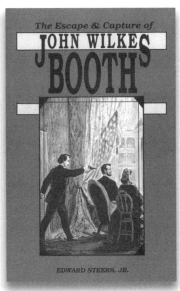

Thomas Publications
ISBN-13: 978-0939631490

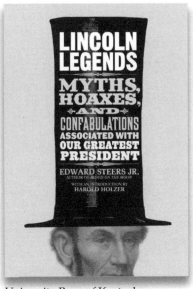

University Press of Kentucky
ISBN-13: 978-0813124667

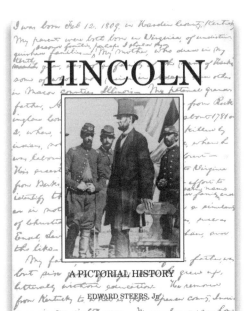

These books are available at bookstores everywhere, or from Amazon.com and other online sources.

Thomas Publications
ISBN-13: 978-157747000